Unified stenography; the simplest and most uniform of any of the Pitmanic systems - Primary Source Edition

Norman Peter Heffley

UNIFIED STENOGRAPHY

THE SIMPLEST AND MOST UNIFORM OF

ANY OF THE PITMANIC SYSTEMS

Prepared for the exclusive use

OF

THE HEFFLEY SCHOOL

Brooklyn-New York

1904

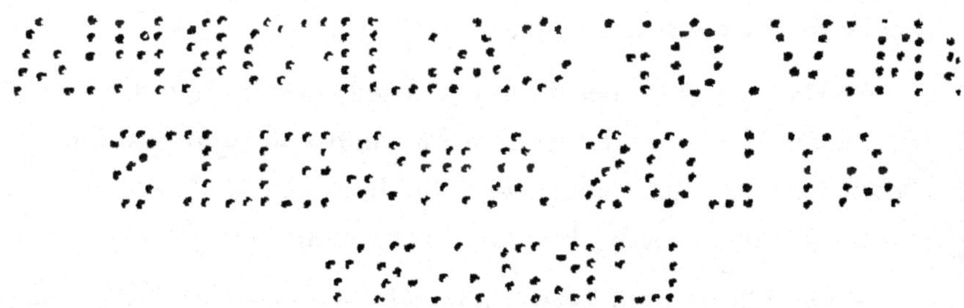

GENERAL DIRECTIONS

The general directions which may be given the student in advance are few, as the principles introduced from time to time in the following pages will be specifically treated, when reference is made to them.

Ruled paper should always be used. Faint red lines are preferable and they should be ruled about one-half inch apart.

Every character must be carefully and correctly formed, and should never be written faster than it can be written well. Ability to write rapidly and legibly will depend upon the precision with which in the beginning each character is written.

Accuracy in writing depends upon the *direction* in which each character is written, its *length*, and whether it is *light* or *heavy*. The perpendicular, slanting, and horizontal strokes should be made in the proper direction, and the curved strokes, when made heavy, should be thickened in the centre only, and should taper toward the extremities; while straight strokes are made heavy throughout, and should be made only sufficiently heavy to distinguish them from light strokes.

Either a pen or a pencil may be used, which should be held between the first and second fingers, in an almost upright position. The notebook must be kept in place with the left hand, and, when one is writing, the weight of the body should not rest upon the right arm.

Everything should be written and read over and over again. Each character, word, or principle must be learned perfectly before the next one is taken up, and nothing outside of the exercises given in connection with each lesson should be attempted. Word-signs must be reviewed daily.

PHONOGRAPHIC ALPHABET

CONSONANTS

Phonograph	*Name*	*Direction written*	*Sound of*		
	P	Downward	P	as in	Pope
	B	"	B	"	babe
	T	"	T	"	tight
	D	"	D	"	dead
	Chay	"	CH	"	church
	J	"	J	"	judge
	K	Left to right	K	"	kick
	Gay	"	G	"	gag
	Ray	Upward	R	"	roar
	Hay	"	H	"	high
	F	Downward	F	"	fife
	V	"	V	"	vat
	Ith	"	TH	"	path
	The	"	TH	"	thy
	S	"	S	"	saw
	Z	"	Z	"	zeal
	Ish	"	SH	"	she
	Zhe	Downward	Z	"	azure / vision
	L / Lay	" / Upward	L	"	lull
	Yay	Downward	Y	"	yet
	R	"	R	"	roar
	Way	"	W	"	wake
	M	Left to right	M	"	maim
	Emp / Emb	" / "	MP / MB	" / "	hemp / ember
	N	"	N	"	noun
	Ing	"	NG	"	thing
	Ink	"	NK	"	think

VOWELS

Sound of		
E	as in	eat
A	"	ate
AH	"	arm
AW	"	all
O	"	oak
OO	"	ooze
ĭ	"	ill
ĕ	"	ell
ă	"	at
ŏ	"	odd
ŭ	"	us
ŏŏ	"	put
I	"	ice
OI	"	oil
OW	"	owl
U	"	use

PHONOGRAPHY

Phonography is based upon a scientific analysis of the sounds of the English language. The common alphabet, as being inadequate for the accurate representation of the various sounds, has been discarded and one more philosophic has been adopted,—one which provides an absolute sign for each consonant and vowel sound.

The CONSONANT signs are derived from the following geometric diagrams:

From these divisions twelve simple straight and curved lines are obtained:

These lines, made light and heavy, are arranged in pairs, the thin strokes representing the whispered sounds, and the heavy strokes the vocal or thickened sounds, as in column 1, on the opposite page.

Each consonant, whether straight or curved, is written in the direction of one of the lines in the following figures:

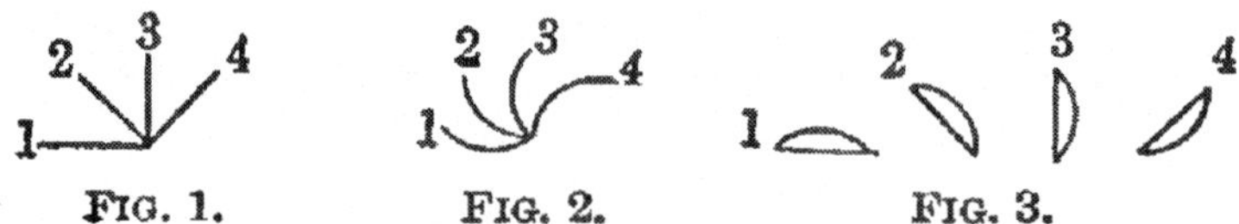

FIG. 1. FIG. 2. FIG. 3.

The lines in the second and fourth directions are inclined exactly midway between the horizontal and perpendicular lines in the first and third directions.

Each sign represents invariably the same *sound*, and is always written in the same direction. (See columns 2 and 3.)

The VOWEL sounds are represented by dots and dashes placed in three positions about the consonant signs, as in column 5.

C O N S O N A N T S

1. Upright and sloping consonants are written DOWNWARD, except lay, ray, and hay, which are written UPWARD.

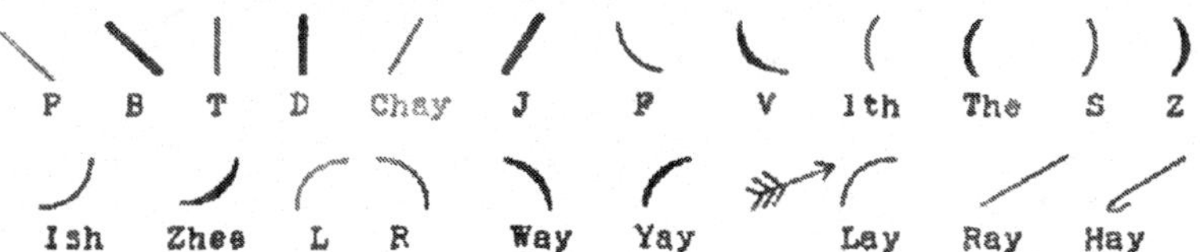

2. Horizontal consonants are written from LEFT to RIGHT.

K Gay M Emp or Emb N Ing or Ink

3. All strokes are made of uniform length. Chay slopes 60, and ray and hay 30, degrees from the line of writing.

Chay Ray Hay

4. When consonants are combined, they are written without lifting the pen from the paper, each succeeding consonant beginning where the preceding one ends.

5. Each consonant is written in the same direction when joined to others as when standing alone. When joined, the first DOWN or UP stroke rests UPON the line. L, when standing alone, is written UPWARD.

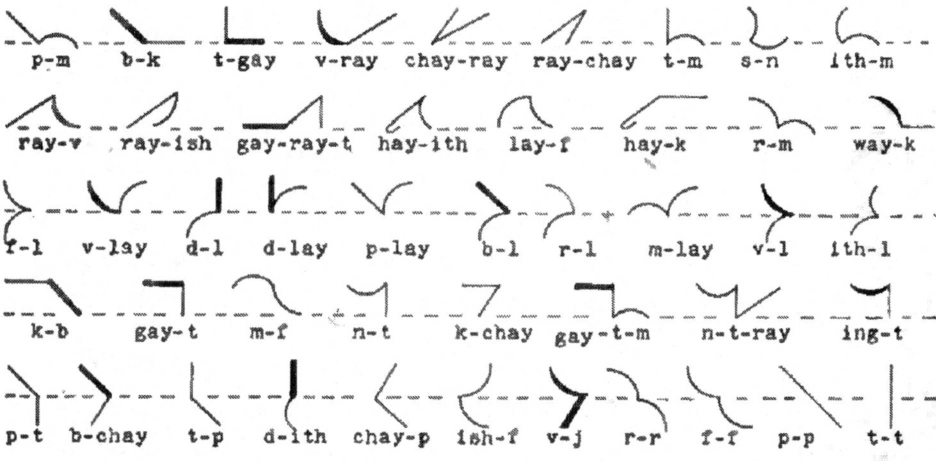

6. Except in a few combinations, an angle is formed between a straight and a curved, and between two curved, consonants.

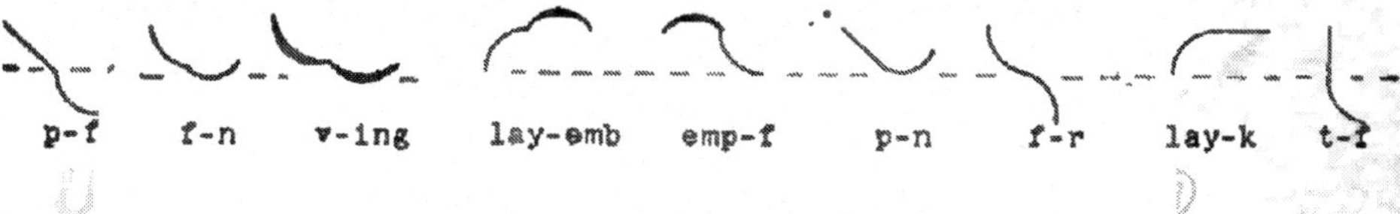

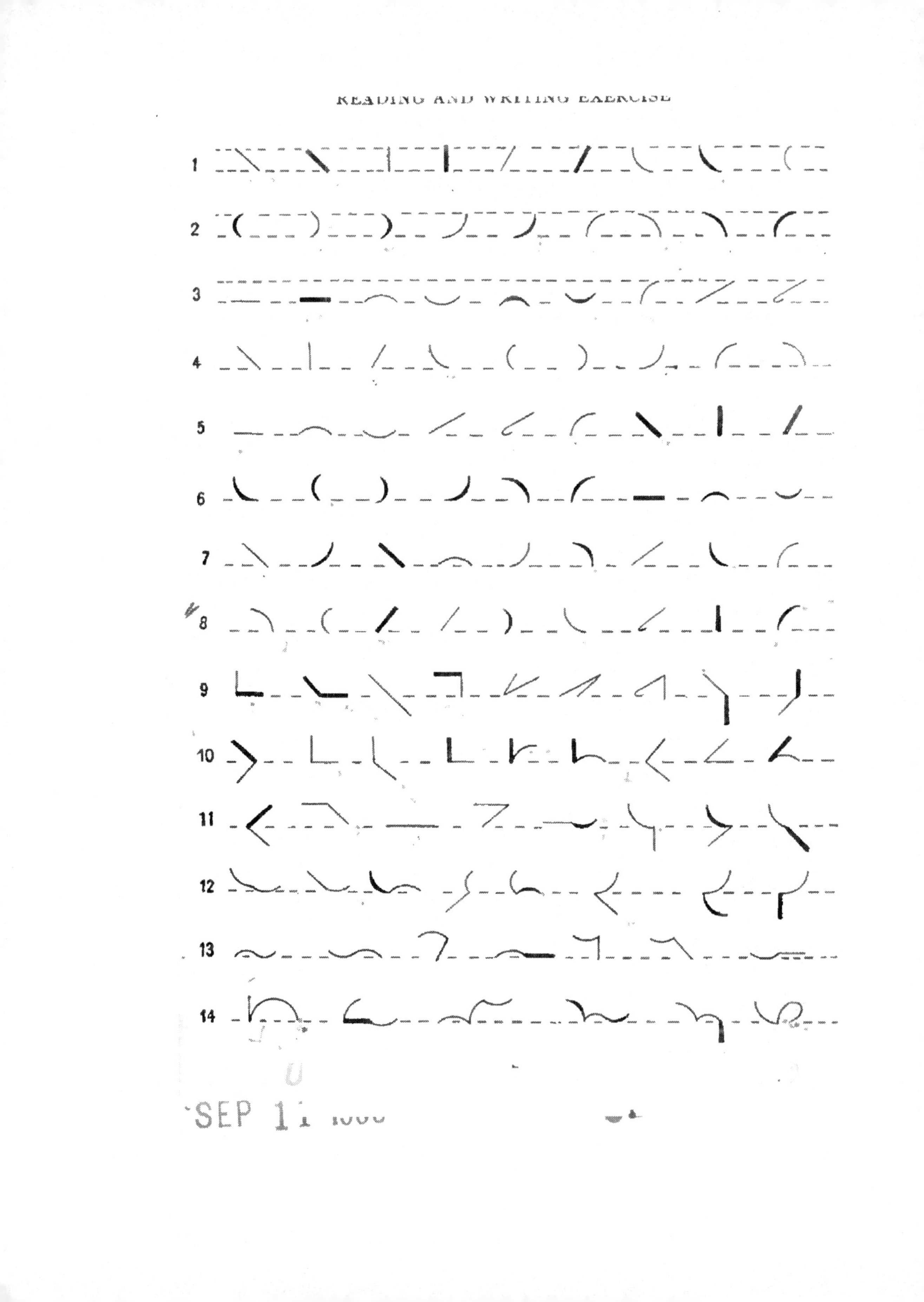

1

2

3

4

5

6

7

8

9

10

11

12

13

14

LONG VOWELS

7. The long-vowel sounds as heard in the words heat, hate, heart, bought, boat, boot, are represented by HEAVY dots and dashes, written at the beginning, middle and end of a consonant.

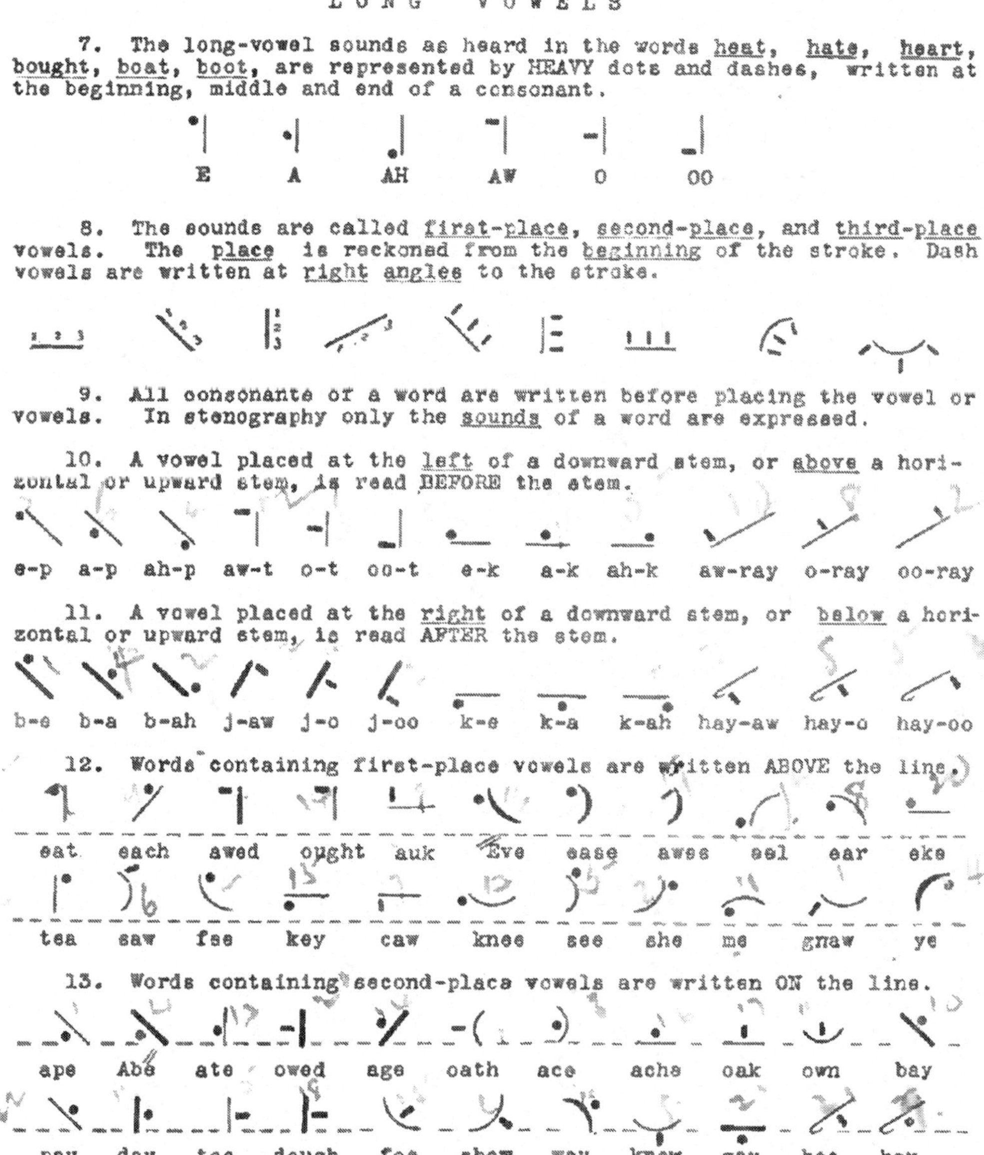

E A AH AW O OO

8. The sounds are called first-place, second-place, and third-place vowels. The place is reckoned from the beginning of the stroke. Dash vowels are written at right angles to the stroke.

9. All consonants of a word are written before placing the vowel or vowels. In stenography only the sounds of a word are expressed.

10. A vowel placed at the left of a downward stem, or above a horizontal or upward stem, is read BEFORE the stem.

e-p a-p ah-p aw-t o-t oo-t e-k a-k ah-k aw-ray o-ray oo-ray

11. A vowel placed at the right of a downward stem, or below a horizontal or upward stem, is read AFTER the stem.

b-e b-a b-ah j-aw j-o j-oo k-e k-a k-ah hay-aw hay-o hay-oo

12. Words containing first-place vowels are written ABOVE the line.

eat each awed ought auk Eve ease awes eel ear eke

tea saw fee key caw knee see she me gnaw ye

13. Words containing second-place vowels are written ON the line.

ape Abe ate owed age oath ace ache oak own bay

pay day toe dough foe show way know gay hoe hay

14. Words containing third-place vowels are written THROUGH the line if downward or upward stems, and UNDER the line if horizontal stems.

ooze boo chew Jew Lou shoe sue woo coo

1

2

3

4

5

6

7

8

9

10

11

12

13

Word signs:

14

The, a, ah, all, too, already, before, owe-oh, ought, who, whom.

SHORT VOWELS

15. The six short-vowel sounds as heard in the words sit, set, sat, lock, luck, look, are represented by light dots and dashes, and written in the same positions and governed by the same rules as the long vowels.

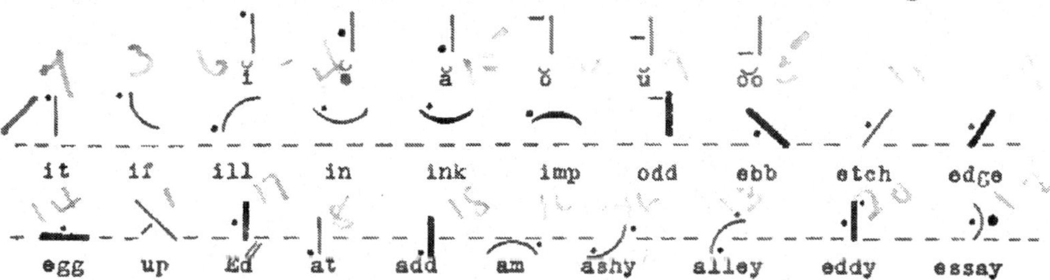

16. A first-place vowel between two consonants is written after the FIRST consonant, second- and third-place vowels are written before the SECOND consonant.

t-e-m t-a-m t-ah-m t-i-p t-e-p t-a-p t-aw-l t-o-l t-oo-l

17. When words contain two or more stems, the first UPWARD or DOWNWARD stem is written in the position of the accented vowel.

talk team balk teach daub sheep tick pitch top tub

bake dome knave thump paid page tape shade duck back

palm doom shook tomb boom Jack tack took book attack

keep cape cap navy gage match meek name camp dump

bought beet boat peach cheap fame shame head peg

buck pump honey shock Edith envy heed dock uncouth

cake keg gag copy canopy Gotham attach vacate

chap dish ditto decay invoke package dado chubby chimney

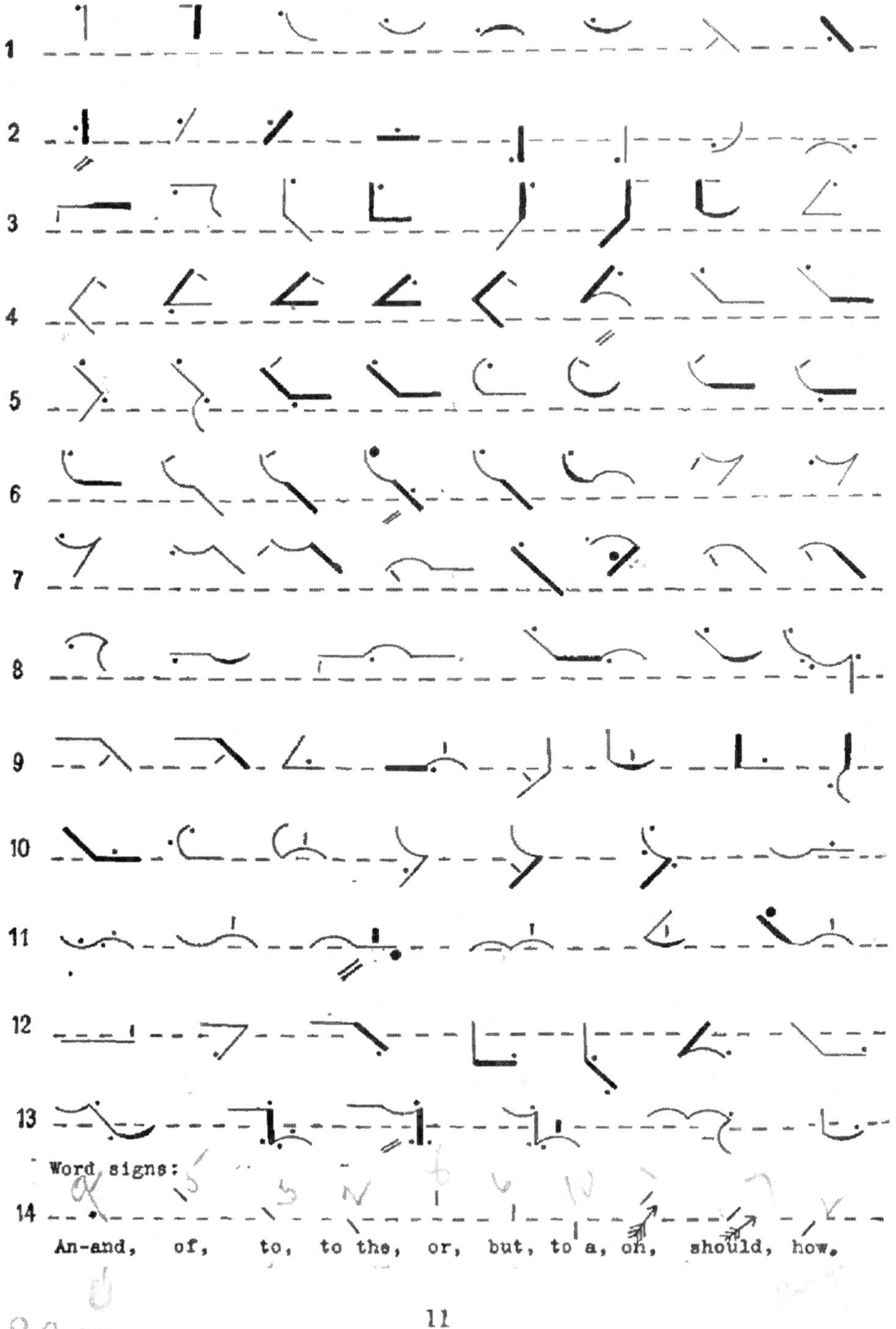
1
2
3
4
5
6
7
8
9
10
11
12
13
Word signs:
14
An-and, of, to, to the, or, but, to a, on, should, how,

DIPHTHONGS

18. The double vowels as heard in the words tie, toy, vow, and view, are expressed as follows:

I OI OW U

19. These signs are always written in the same direction, and may be joined to the stem if they form an acute angle.

pie thy type knife toy boy decoy out our couch use

eyes Ida item oil oily bow vow thou endow few view

20. When two vowels occur between two consonants, write the first vowel after the first consonant and the second vowel before the second consonant.

poem payer weigher gayety deity fuel vowel power bower

21. When two vowels either precede or follow a consonant, that vowel which is to be read next the consonant is written nearer to it.

iota idea payee boa Iowa Genoa Padua radii avowee

22. When the SOUND of L or R begins a word, lay or ray is used; when it ends a word l or r is used.

law lay leap lake like wrought rug rub ray rope ring

feel pail ball call coal bear share pier pour

Exceptions: L or R is used before M or Emp, and Lay or Ray is used after M, Emp, or Ray.

Rome loom ream limp mail meal rail reel

23. When the SOUND of L or R follows an initial vowel sound, L or R is used; when it precedes a final vowel sound, Lay or Ray is used.

elm elk alumn elect alike era air ore ark arm

pillow delay fellow valley hourly Peru Harry carry bureau

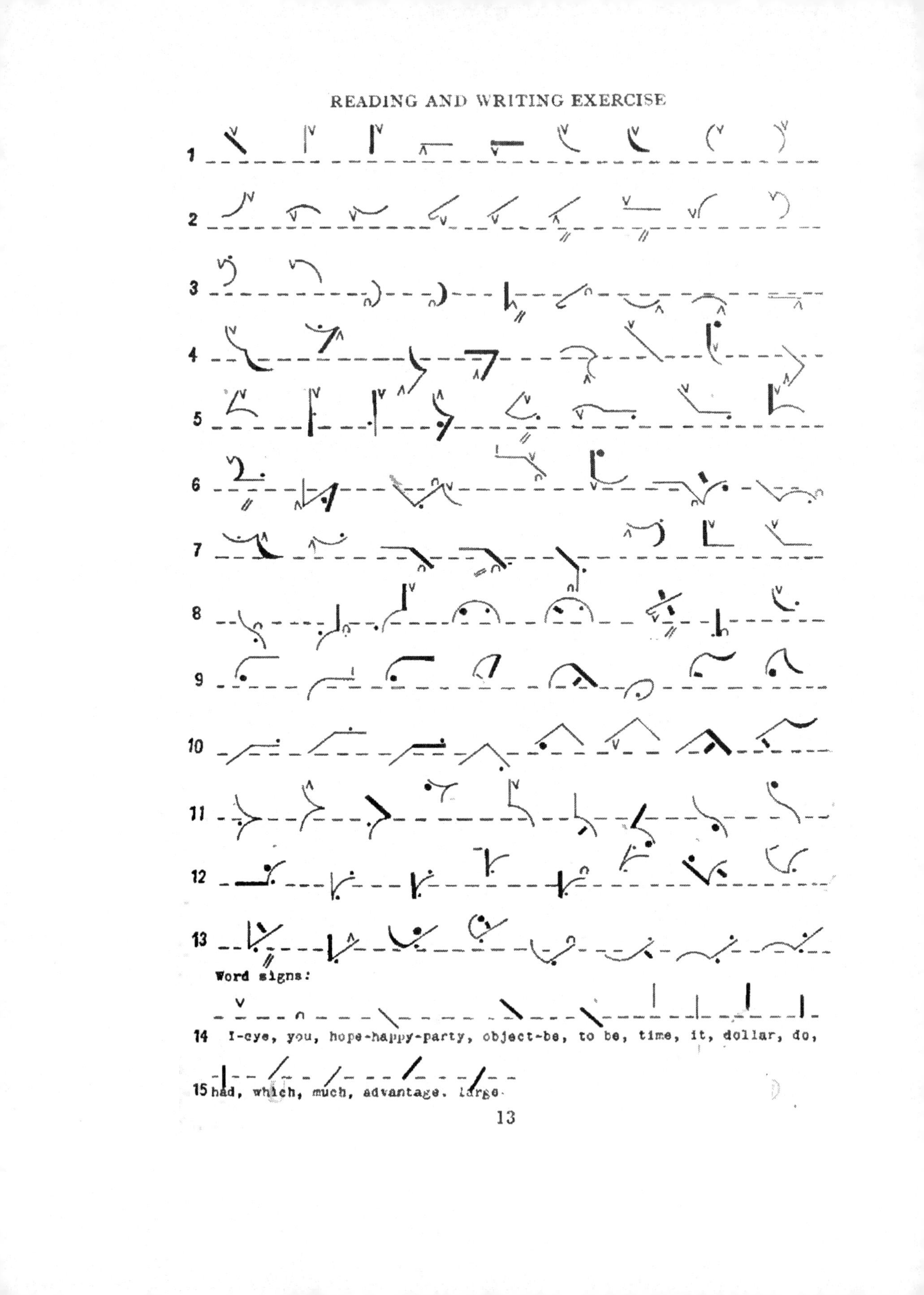

READING AND WRITING EXERCISE

1

2

3

4

5

6

7

8

9

10

11

12

13

Word signs:

14 I-eye, you, hope-happy-party, object-be, to be, time, it, dollar, do,

15 had, which, much, advantage, large.

C I R C L E S or Z.

24. S and Z are also represented by a small INITIAL or FINAL circle, called Iss. It is written on the RIGHT-HAND side of downward straight strokes, and on the UPPER side of horizontal and upward straight strokes. It is written on the INSIDE of curved strokes.

It is read FIRST when it begins and LAST when it ends an outline.

iss-k iss-b iss-t iss-chay iss-ray iss-f iss-ith iss-s iss-r iss-n iss-m

gay-iss b-iss d-iss j-iss hay-iss v-iss s-iss way-iss m-iss n-iss emp-iss

25. The circle is written on the OUTSIDE of the angle formed by straight strokes. Between other consonants it is written in the more convenient way.

t-iss-k gay-iss-t chay-iss-k b-iss-f p-iss-r f-iss-n n-iss-m m-iss-lay

26. The circle form is used for all words that BEGIN with S, or that END with S or Z.

sight soap sake said such spoke sorrow slow save sash sing sark

base dies chase choose less miss news stays sales suns notice

desk cask reason Cincinnati business Missouri justices succeeds

27. The stroke form is used: (a) For all words that BEGIN with Z. (b) For all words in which S or Z follows an initial vowel sound, or precedes a final vowel sound. (c) For all words in which two vowels follow an initial S or Z, or precede a final S or Z.

(a) Czar zero zealous zinc (b) icy assume acid Isaac busy daisy

noisy agency Tasso (c) Zion science sower Siam chaos pious bias

28. The sounds of SES, SEZ, ZES, ZEZ, are represented by a circle twice the size of the iss circle. It is called sez and is used in the same way as the iss circle.

paces tenses cases voices noises looses amazes sources forces successive

29. S may follow the sez circle by an additional small circle.

abscesses excesses successes recesses possesses dispossesses

READING AND WRITING EXERCISE

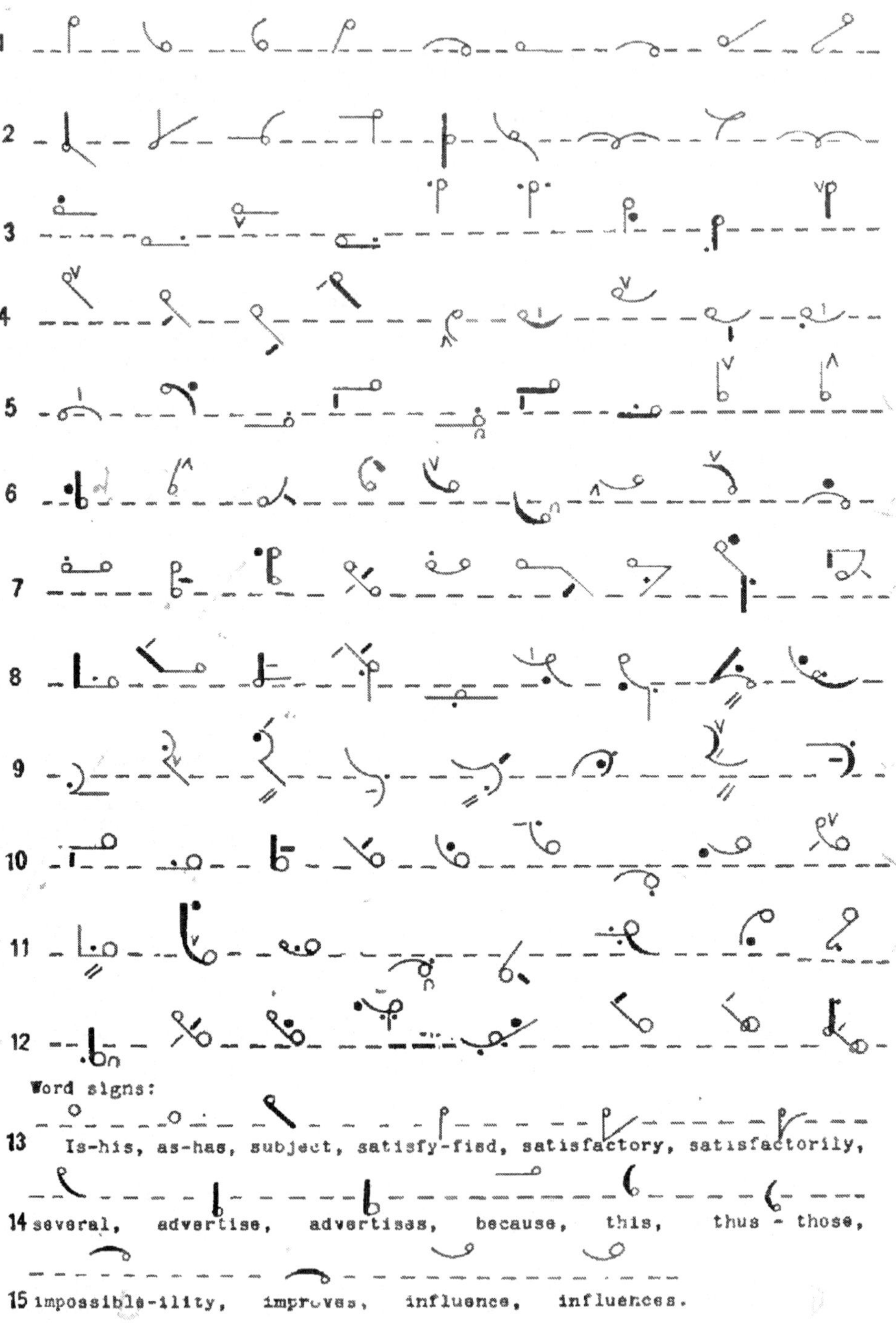

THE IST and STER LOOPS

30. St is expressed by a small initial or final loop. It is made one half the length of the stem. It is written on the circle side and is governed by the same rules as apply to the iss circle.

steep stub state stout stood steady stitch stage stake stick

stiff staff stove stave steal stale steam stall stem stamp

post passed best based tossed dust chest just cast guest rest

feast fast vast zest list lost missed most west waste yeast

amassed assist assessed arrest jest honest store story star

destiny tallest ballast utmost tempest reduced revised refused

rejoiced unjust coolest calmest artistic testify justify mystify

taste tasty haste hasty must musty rust rusty mist misty steamy

31. Str is represented by a large final loop two thirds the length of the stroke. It is treated in the same way as the final ist loop.

poster teeter duster jester coaster castor Rochester foster vaster

lustre arrester disturb nestor Worcester impostor songster yesterday

32. S may follow the loops by making an additional small circle.

lists boasts toasts tests lasts costs coasts ghosts wrists rusts

nests invests jests feasters masters Lester's musters teamsters

dusters disasters gamesters songsters boasters ministers

READING AND WRITING EXERCISE

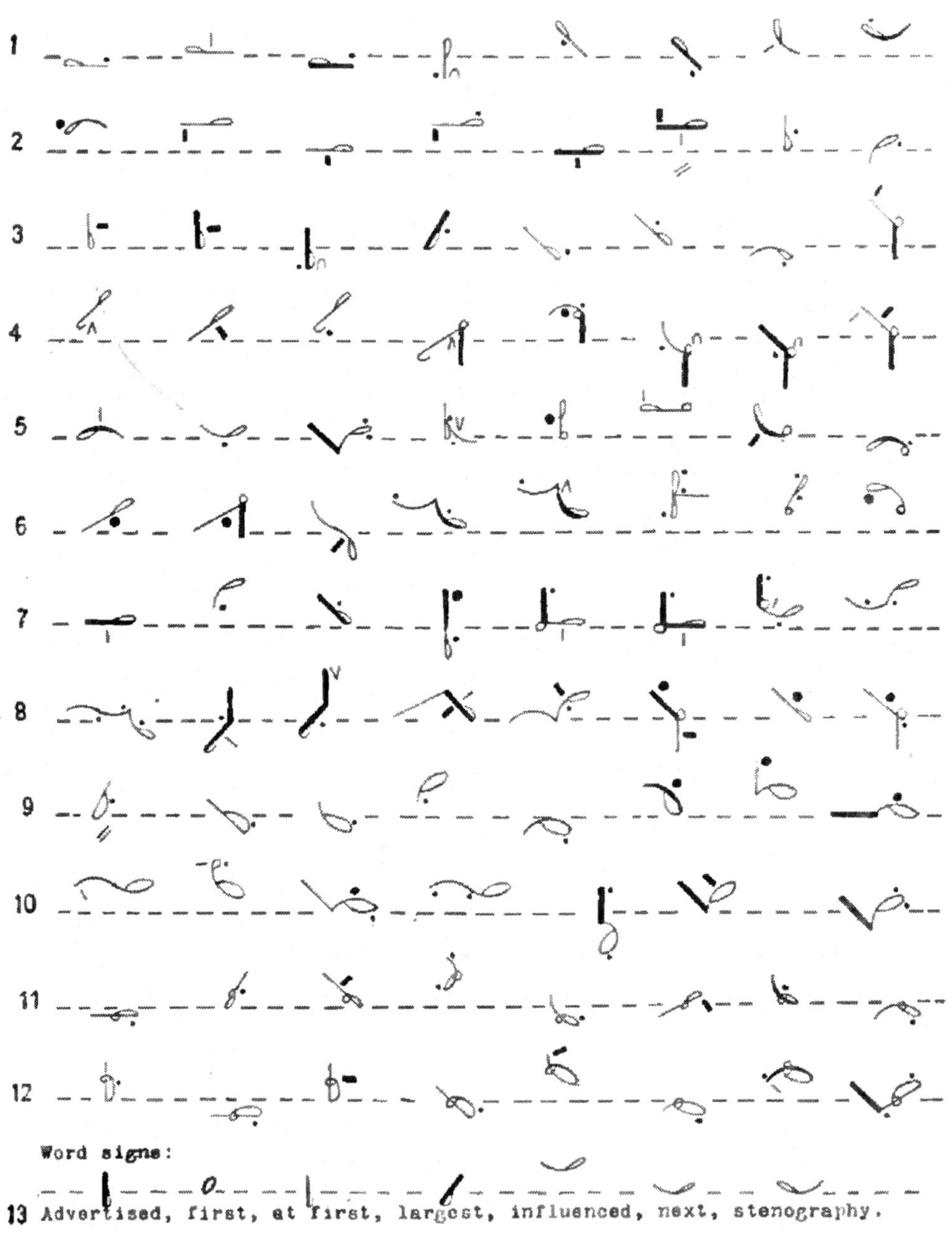

Word signs:

13 Advertised, first, at first, largest, influenced, next, stenography.

W and Y

33. Small INITIAL semicircles, called <u>weh</u> and <u>yeh</u>, respectively, are also used to indicate W and Y. The semicircle for W may open either to the <u>right</u> or <u>left</u>; that for Y either <u>upward</u> or <u>downward</u>. That one should be used which makes the better angle with the stem.

The rules governing the use of the initial circle <u>s</u> apply to the semicircles.

web wade wide widow weep weighed wedge walk woke woof wages

wives wove weaves wash wax weds weights wade wing wife waif

wore wear weery wire waive warm weary worth worthy DeWitt

youth yoke yachts Yale yellow young Yates yokes Europe Yankee

woe away awake awoke Wyoming Oswego wise wiser Oyer yee yeas

34. A LARGE initial hook on the <u>circle side</u> of T, D, K, and Gay, forming the double consonants <u>tway</u>, <u>dway</u>, <u>kway</u>, and <u>gway</u>, is used to represent W. They are vowelized the same as simple stems.

twill twice dwell quite quit quip quire require inquire inquiry

35. S may precede the semicircle and the <u>w</u> hook by making the circle <u>inside</u> of the semicircle or hook.

sweep Swede switch swung swing squaw squeeze square squad sequel

THE ASPIRATE H

36. H is also expressed by a short, light, initial tick, called <u>heh</u>. It is written in the direction of T or K and is always read first.

head hatch hedge hook hazy Hague hero harrass horrify hive hath

howl here why ham hemp hung hogshead unhook white whit whim

Note: <u>WH</u> at the beginning of words is sounded as <u>HW</u>, which sound is represented by the thickened semicircle for <u>W</u>.

READING AND WRITING EXERCISE

1

2

3

4

5

6

7

8

9

10

11

12

Word signs:

13 He-him, we-with, were, what, would, year, yet, beyond, you, that, when, aware.

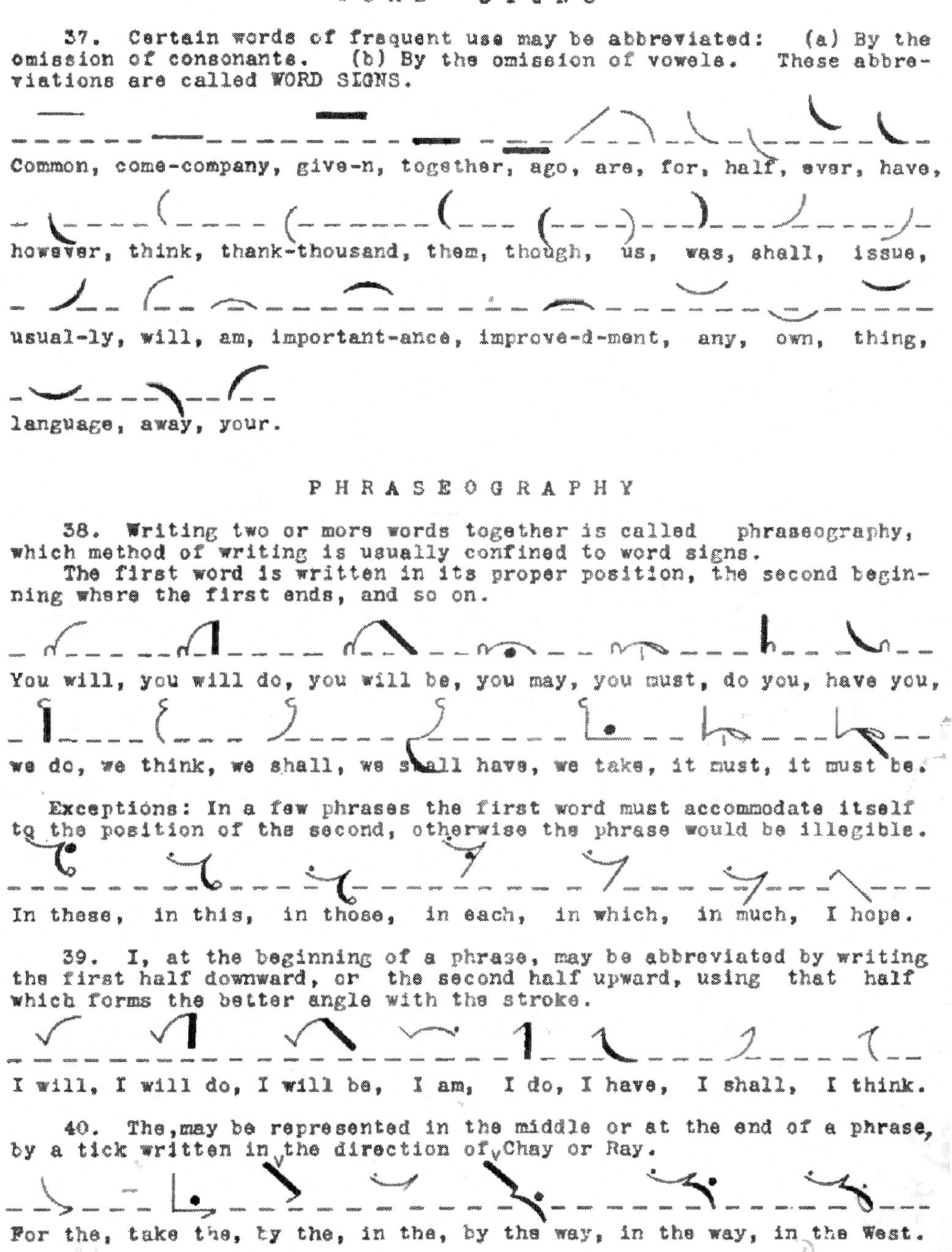

W O R D   S I G N S

37. Certain words of frequent use may be abbreviated: (a) By the omission of consonante. (b) By the omission of vowels. These abbreviations are called WORD SIGNS.

Common, come-company, give-n, together, ago, are, for, half, ever, have,

however, think, thank-thousand, them, though, us, was, shall, issue,

usual-ly, will, am, important-ance, improve-d-ment, any, own, thing,

language, away, your.

P H R A S E O G R A P H Y

38. Writing two or more words together is called phraseography, which method of writing is usually confined to word signs.
The first word is written in its proper position, the second beginning where the first ends, and so on.

You will, you will do, you will be, you may, you must, do you, have you,

we do, we think, we shall, we shall have, we take, it must, it must be.

Exceptions: In a few phrases the first word must accommodate itself to the position of the second, otherwise the phrase would be illegible.

In these, in this, in those, in each, in which, in much, I hope.

39. I, at the beginning of a phrase, may be abbreviated by writing the first half downward, or the second half upward, using that half which forms the better angle with the stroke.

I will, I will do, I will be, I am, I do, I have, I shall, I think.

40. The, may be represented in the middle or at the end of a phrase, by a tick written in the direction of Chay or Ray.

For the, take the, by the, in the, by the way, in the way, in the West.

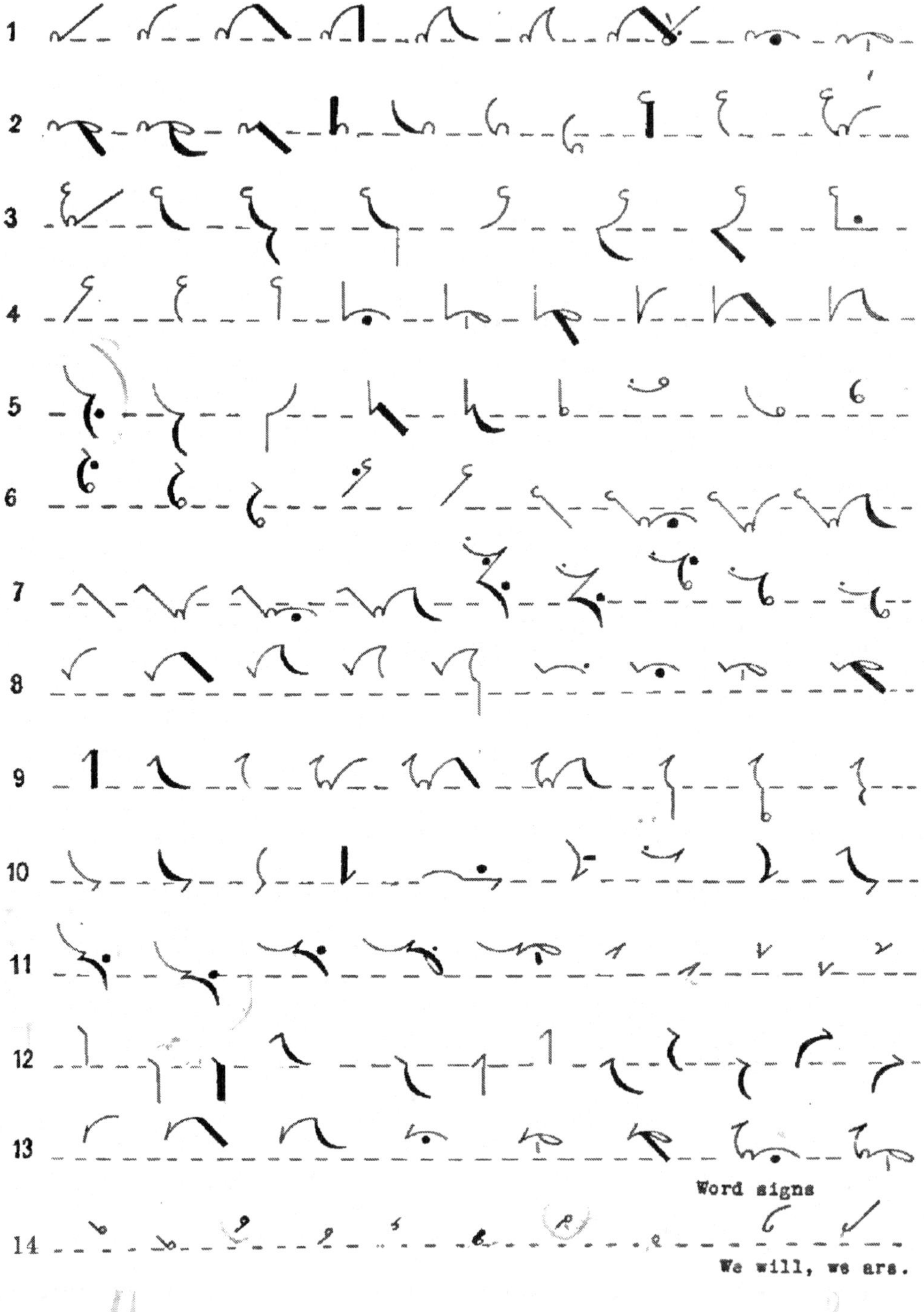
1
2
3
4
5
6
7
8
9
10
11
12
13
Word signs
14
We will, we are.

THE R HOOK

41. An additional sign for R is supplied by a small INITIAL hook opposite the circle side of straight strokes, and on the inside of curved strokes.

per ber ter der cher jer ker ger fer ver ther ther sher

zher ler yer rer wer mer ner emper or ember inger or inker

42. The r hook is pronounced with the consonant, as per, ber, etc., and not as P-R, B-R, etc. The combined stem and hook, which is called a double consonant, is vowelized the same as a simple stem.

pry pray Troy true dray cry free fry throw three through shrew

outer utter etcher acre eager either humor honor author usher

tinker rancor anchor longer younger lumber franker finger linger

trees grows breaks drips creeps shrieks shrubs primes bribes

powder maker nailer banner collar proffer jobber robber vigor labor

paupers bakers teechers wagers batteries wreckers mockers Christmas

43. S must precede the r hook on straight letters by making the hook into a circle. On curved letters it is made inside of the hook.

spray spruce spry suppress seeker solder spring strike suffer simmer

expressly destroy extreme westerly prosper stronger designer deciphers

44. Skr or sgr following d, p, or b; and spr or sbr, following j, are formed as follows:

disgrace disagrees jasper prescribe subscribe subscriber

1

2

3

4

5

6

7

8

9

10

11

12

Word signs:

13

Appear, principle-al-ly, practice, member-remember, number,

14

doctor, dear, during danger, larger, degree. from

THE L HOOK

45. L may also be represented by a SMALL initial hook, on the circle side of straight strokes, and by a LARGE initial hook on the inside of curved strokes.

pel bel tel del chel jel kel gel rel fel vel thel thel sel zel

shel zhel lel yel rel wel mel nel empel or embel ingel or inkel

46. The rules that govern the use of the stems with the r hook attached apply to those with the l hook.

idle able apple addle eagle Ethel oval evil awful uncle easel

ply play blow blue clay claw glue flee fly flow flew flaw

Bible title total tackle double chapel baffle bevel cobble regal

reply bottle fickle vocal knuckle legal illegal panel tunnel

funnel enamel bushel official pearl girl rural choral rouble

trouble trifle prattle blacker plumper plural clamor floral nailer

place applause angles close staple stable replace pleased closed

struggle pickles rubbers blooms pupils clauses classes pleases

47. S may precede the l hook by making the circle within the hook.

supply splice sable subtle settle satchel sickle civil sooner

possible bicycle display displace disclose physical plausible

blissful classical explosive noticeable dissemble feasible exclusive

READING AND WRITING EXERCISE

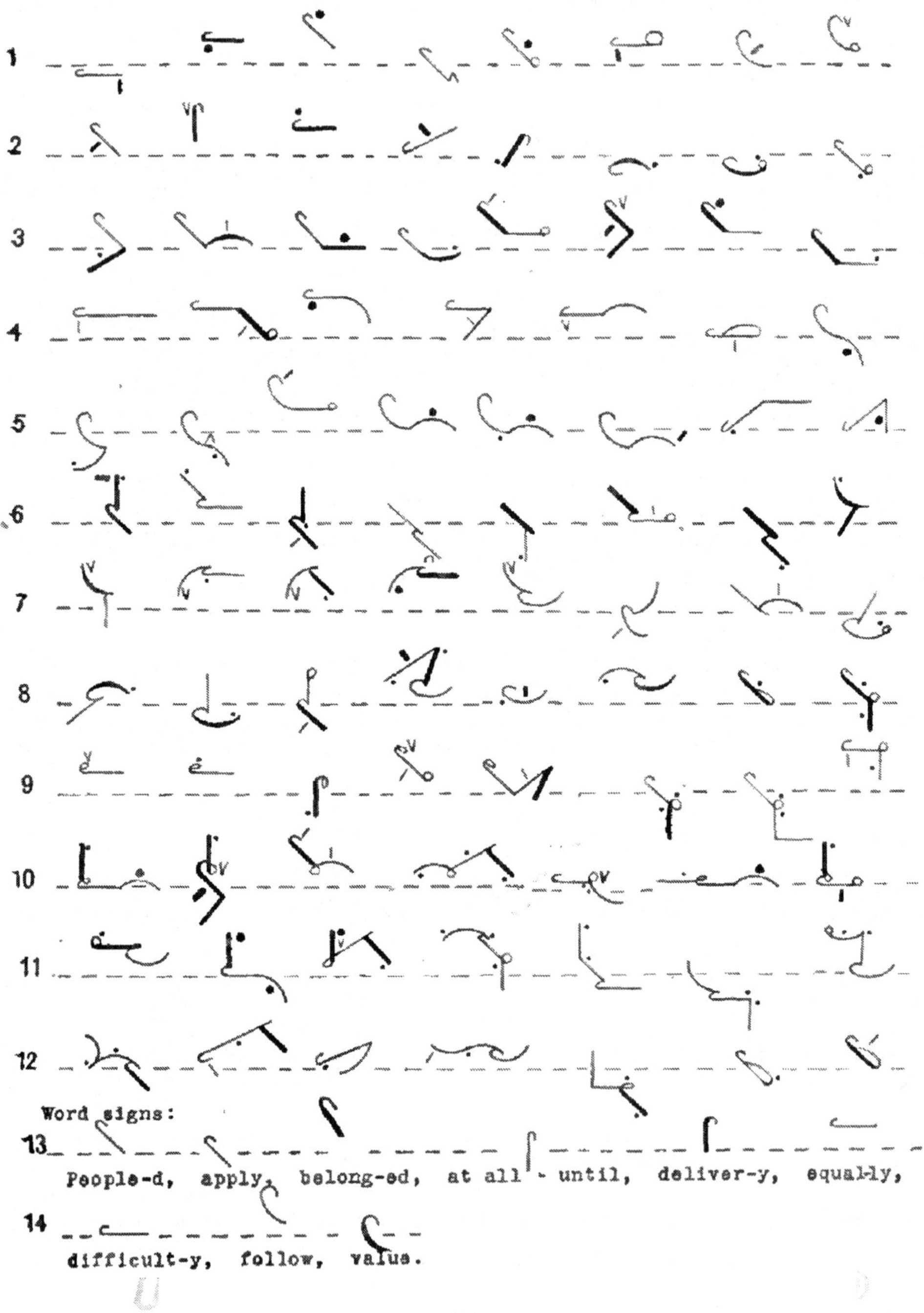

T H E   N   H O O K

48. A small FINAL hook opposite the circle side of straight, and on the inside of curved strokes, represents N.

pine bane ton down chain join can gain rain hen fun vain thin

than zone shun lean earn mine known fine hone impugn heaven

human iron ocean often evening refine banish plenty twenty finish

finance Bayonne bayonet money many funny Diana peon ruin lion

49. S, ses, ist, and ster are written on the n-hook side of straight letters to represent final ns, nses, nst, or nstr. A circle may be added to the loops for a final S.

pains towns dines trains strains brains queens hence turns stones

dances princes trances chances Kansas glances expenses essences

pounced against pranced pronoun pronounced punster punsters

50. On curved letters, the circle is written in the hook for final S.

vines loans moans frowns shrines remonstrance evinces announces

T H E   F or V   H O O K

51. A small FINAL hook on the circle side of straight stems adds F or V.

tough dove chief gave roof heave grove strife refer reference

defense driven discovery behave achieve cover reserve govern Tiffany

paves [illegible] drives derives gloves observe refuse trophy surveys

READING AND WRITING EXERCISE

1

2

3

4

5

6

7

8

9

10

11

Word signs:

12

general-ly, can, begin, phonography, opinion, our own, your own,

13 at length, at once, generals-ize, generalized, remembrance, differ-ent-ence,

14 advance-d, careful-ly, hope to have, whatever, out of, whichever, whoever.

THE S H U N HOOK

52. The syllable shun is represented by a LARGE final hook on either side of straight letters and on the inside of curved letters.

option passion addition auction occasion fashion evasion session

illusion oration ration emotion notion unction education adoption

admission delusion fiction function location erection ammunition

notation educational sectional petitioner auctioneer dictionary

national visionary attention application ambition operation intimation

53. S, following the shun hook, is made inside of the hook.

potions editions actions visions allusions litigations sanctions

motions ovations lotions nations notations ascensions junctions

THE S-SHUN HOOK

54. Shun is also expressed by a SMALL hook following the s or ns circle. A first-place vowel occurring between the s and shun is written at the beginning of the hook, and a second-place vowel is written at the end of the hook. The hook-vowel does not govern the word-position.

opposition oppositional possession accession precision procession

decision physician cessation musician supposition processional

55. S may follow the s-shun hook by writing the circle inside of the hook.

positions dispensations expositions acquisitions transitions

depositions impositions civilizations propositions sensations

READING AND WRITING EXERCISE

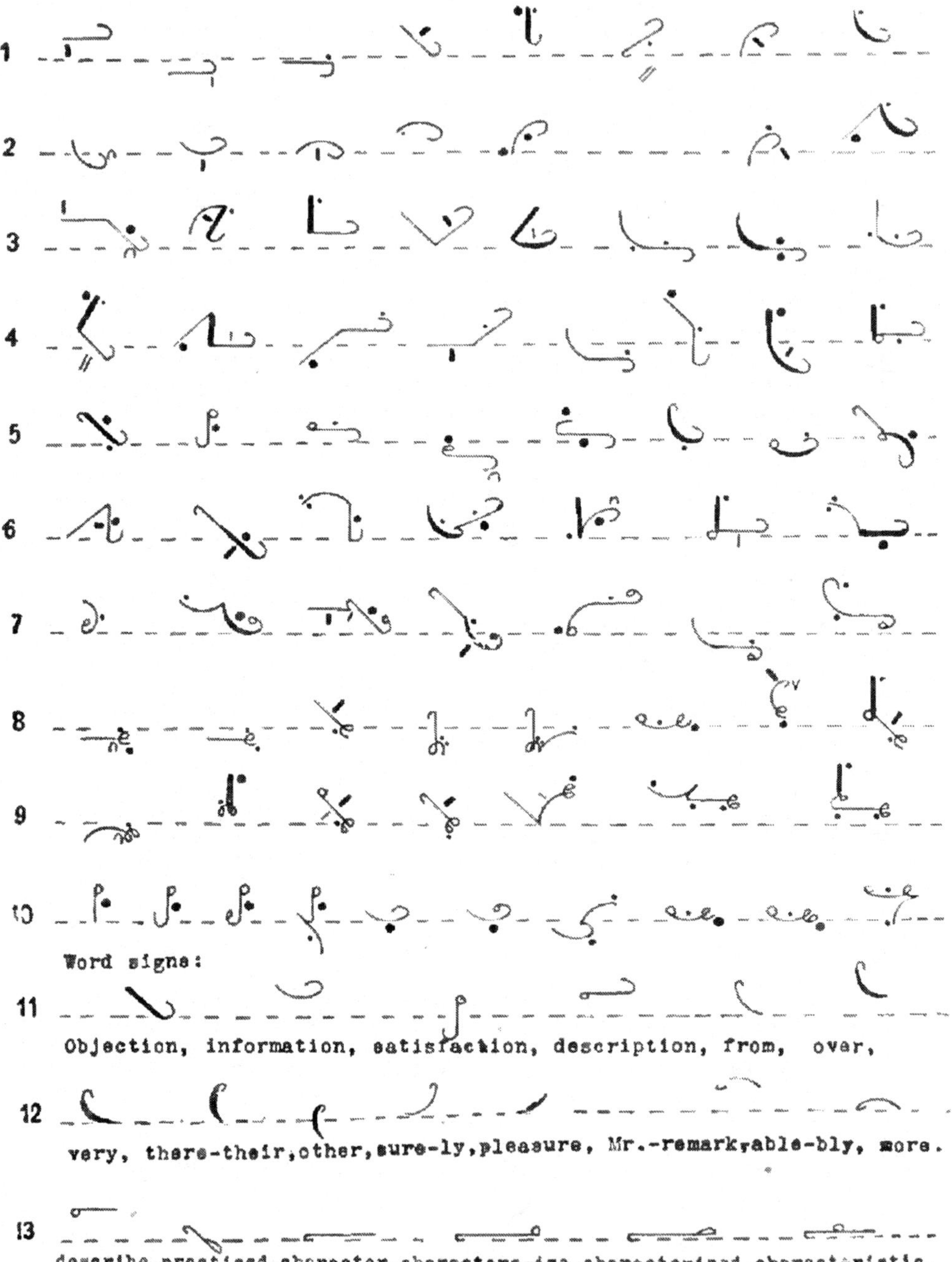

ADDED T OR D.

56. By writing a stroke consonant HALF its usual length, T or D is added:

(a) T is added to light, and D to heavy, SIMPLE strokes.

(b) T or D is added to COMPOUND characters, or to a simple stroke written with another stroke.

The added sound is read after the stem and after all vowels and hooks, but before the final circle. The outlines are written above, on and below the line.

tight fight late art might neat sent sapped spite pits feats

deed died jade egged void vowed viewed couch couched chalked

wend wind achieved tent dined brightly heartily betrayed talkative

pride plate bent band blend tends prints braids faints gifts

57. D is added to the simple strokes m and n by making them heavy. The simple strokes ray, emp and ing, are not halved when standing alone. Compound characters are stems with hooks or the semicircle.

made mad aimed seemed end send signed sound need ends

58. The final syllable ted or ded is expressed by a half-length T or D; disjoined if necessary.

coated evaded noted ended intended counted fainted dated offended

SUFFIXES

59. Ing is represented by a light dot, ings by a small circle, and ing the by the chetoid tick written at the end of a word.

paying buying trying screening having thinking shining speaking

doings meetings drawings engravings trying the taking the saving the

60. Ility, ality, and arity are expressed by disjoining the consonant that comes immediately before the ility, etc., and writing it close to the preceding part of the word.

suitability stability responsibility formality prosperity popularity

1

2

3

4

5

6

7

8

9

10

11

Word signs:

12

Particular-ly, opportunity, part, remembered, at hand, did not, do not,

13

had not, gentlemen, gentleman, quite, could, good, that, without,

14

immediate-ly, under, hand - owned, somewhat.

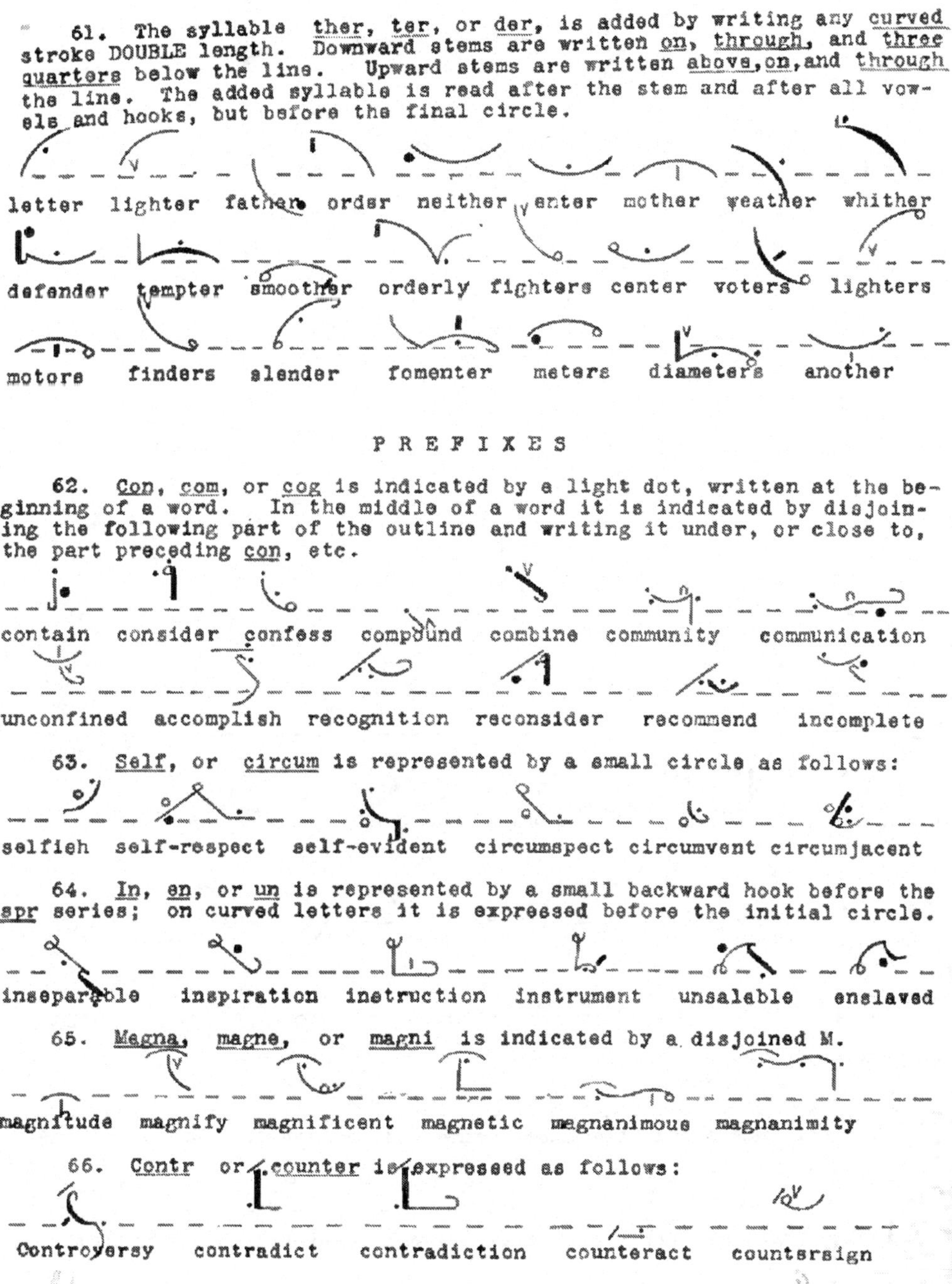

ADDED THER, TER, OR DER.

61. The syllable <u>ther</u>, <u>ter</u>, or <u>der</u>, is added by writing any <u>curved</u> stroke DOUBLE length. Downward stems are written <u>on</u>, <u>through</u>, and <u>three quarters</u> below the line. Upward stems are written <u>above</u>, <u>on</u>, and <u>through</u> the line. The added syllable is read after the stem and after all vowels and hooks, but before the final circle.

P R E F I X E S

62. <u>Con</u>, <u>com</u>, or <u>cog</u> is indicated by a light dot, written at the beginning of a word. In the middle of a word it is indicated by disjoining the following part of the outline and writing it under, or close to, the part preceding <u>con</u>, etc.

63. <u>Self</u>, or <u>circum</u> is represented by a small circle as follows:

64. <u>In</u>, <u>en</u>, or <u>un</u> is represented by a small backward hook before the <u>spr</u> series; on curved letters it is expressed before the initial circle.

65. <u>Magna</u>, <u>magne</u>, or <u>magni</u> is indicated by a disjoined M.

66. <u>Contr</u> or <u>counter</u> is expressed as follows:

READING AND WRITING EXERCISE

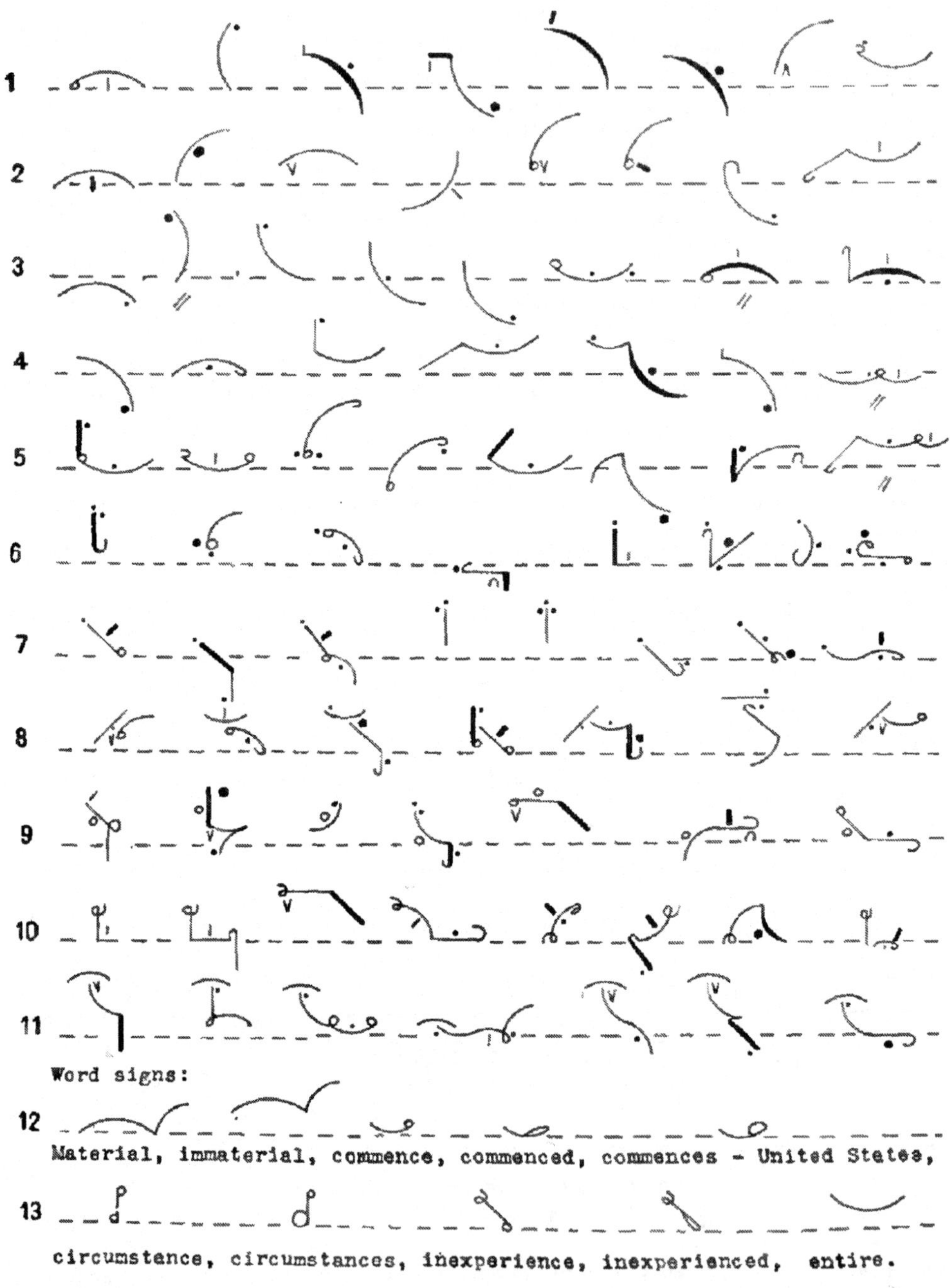

Word signs:

12 Material, immaterial, commence, commenced, commences - United States,

13 circumstence, circumstances, inexperience, inexperienced, entire.

S P E C I A L   V O C A L I Z A T I O N

67. The vowel sound used in connection with the <u>ses</u> circle is the short second place dot. Other vowel sounds may be indicated by writing the sign <u>within</u> the circle.

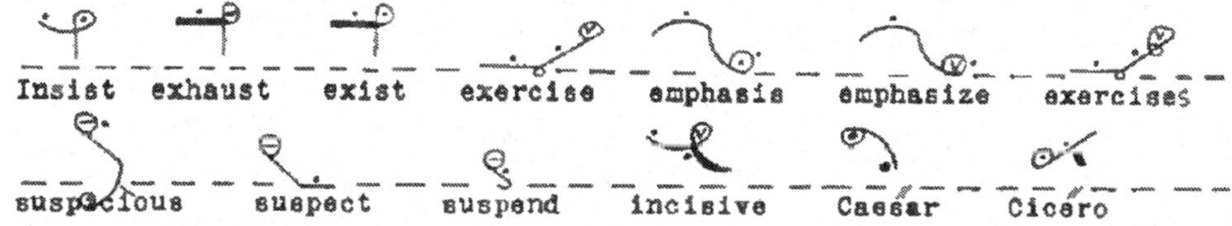

68. Occasionally vowels may be expressed between the stem and the <u>l</u> or <u>r</u> hooks, as follows:

(a) Make a small circle <u>before</u> the stroke for the long dot vowels, and <u>after</u> the stroke for the short dot vowels.

(b) First-place dash vowels and diphthongs are written <u>before</u> or <u>over</u> the hook; second- and third-place dash vowels or diphthongs are written <u>through</u> the stem in their respective places.

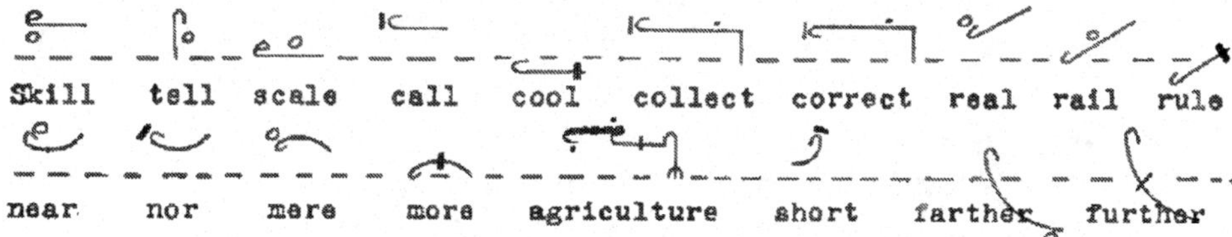

69. The final syllable <u>ly</u>, may be disjoined when it does not form an angle with the preceding part of the word.

Plainly blindly kindly manly justly heavenly

70. The circle <u>iss</u> may be added to words or word signs to form the plural number or possessive case. <u>Lay</u>, may also be added to words, or word signs for the final syllable <u>ly</u>.

71. Word signs, joined or disjoined, may be used as parts of words.

READING AND WRITING EXERCISE

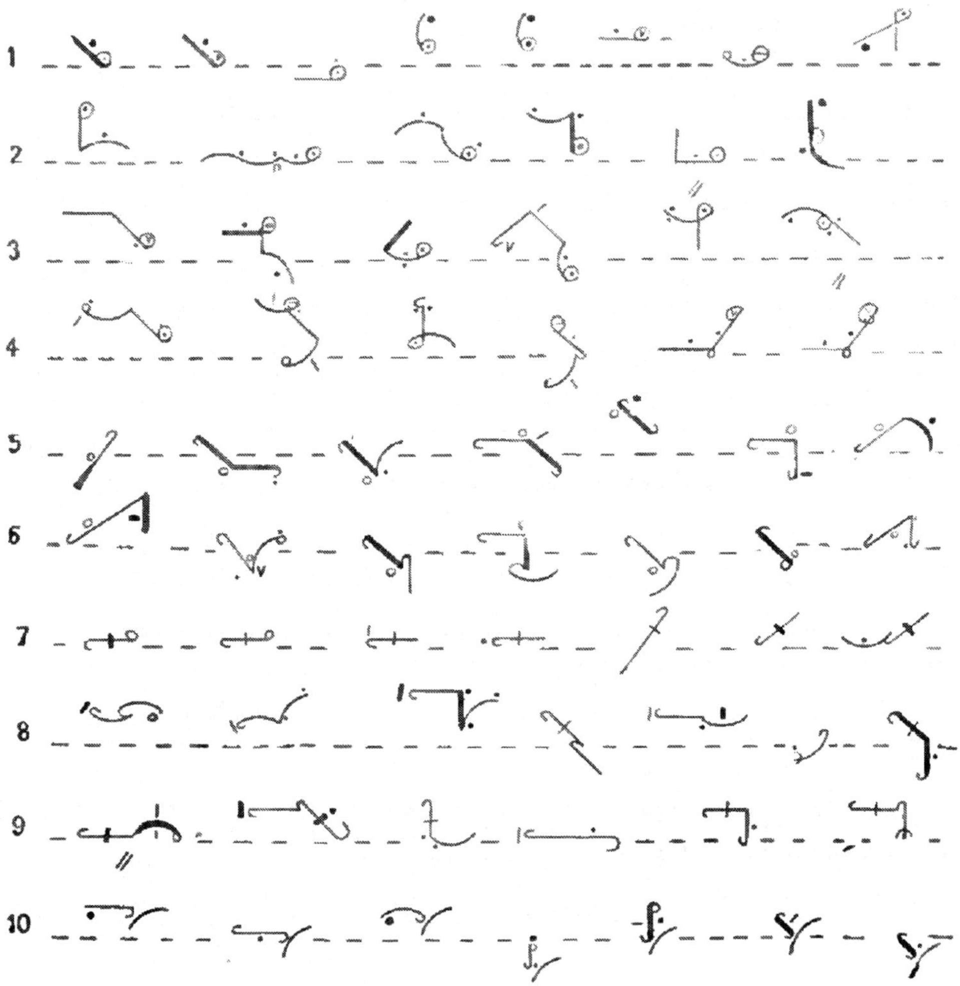

1

2

3

4

5

6

7

8

9

10

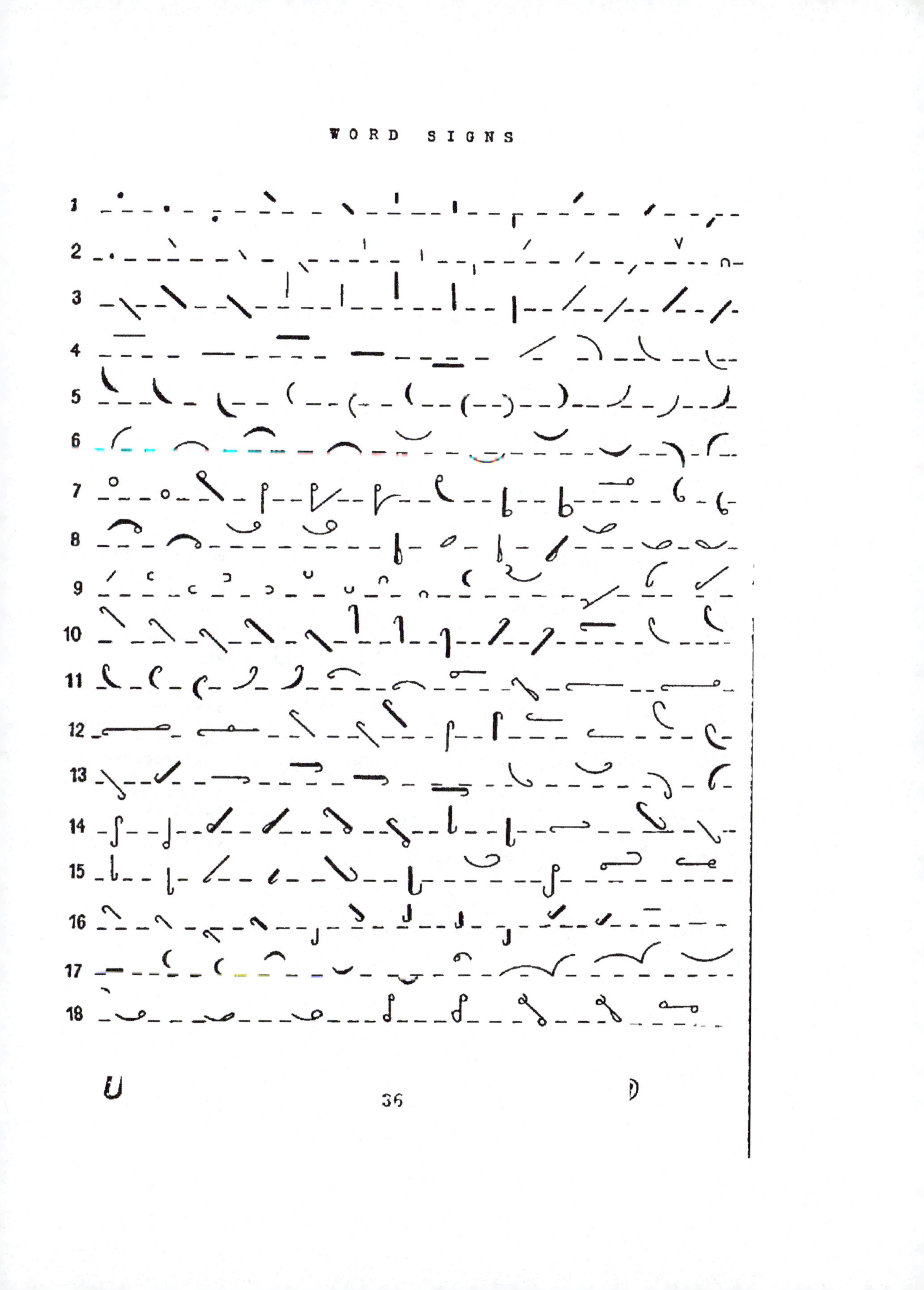

WORD SIGNS

1

2

3

4

5

6

7

8

9

10

11

12

13

14

15

16

17

18

WORD-SIGN WORDS

Portions of the following words are composed of one or more word signs.

Advancement
afterward
altogether
anybody
anyhow
anything
awe
become
disadvantage
enlarge-d
foreclose
foreclosure
forever
forward
hereafter
hereinafter
misunderstand
misunderstood
nobody
objectionable

onward
owing
subjected
to-day
to-morrow
undersell
undersign
undersigned
underwriter
whatsoever
whensoever
whereas
wheresoever
whereupon
wherever
whichsoever
whosoever
withdraw
withheld
withstand

Yourself, myself, himself, themselves, ourselves, yourselves.

O U T L I N E S

In order to write with the rapidity of speech, words can be represented only by their consonant outlines, although occasionally it may be necessary to insert vowels. As a majority of the consonant letters are formed in two or more ways, many words may be written with several different outlines.

The principal guide to the selection of outlines is that of <u>convenience</u> and <u>ease</u> in writing. How to make this selection, aside from the word signs and the words in the following lists, must be left to the stenographer. To qualify him for this selection it is absolutely necessary that he should possess a thorough knowledge of the principles as given in the previous lessons. If he does not possess this knowledge he should review the work before proceeding further.

Each principle must be thoroughly learned and applied before facility will be acquired for writing from miscellaneous matter.

WORDS DISTINGUISHED BY DIFFERENCE IN OUTLINE

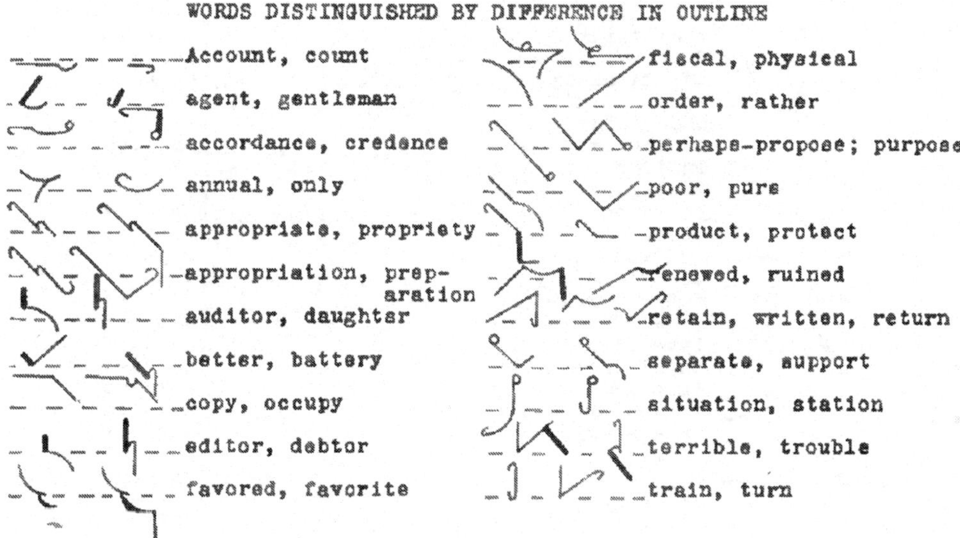

C O N T R A C T E D   W O R D S

The outlines of the following words, because of their awkward forms when written in full, are contracted by writing only their prominent consonants. These are called "Contractions." The outlines are generally suggestive of the words they represent, but they should be thoroughly memorized so that they may be written without hesitation.

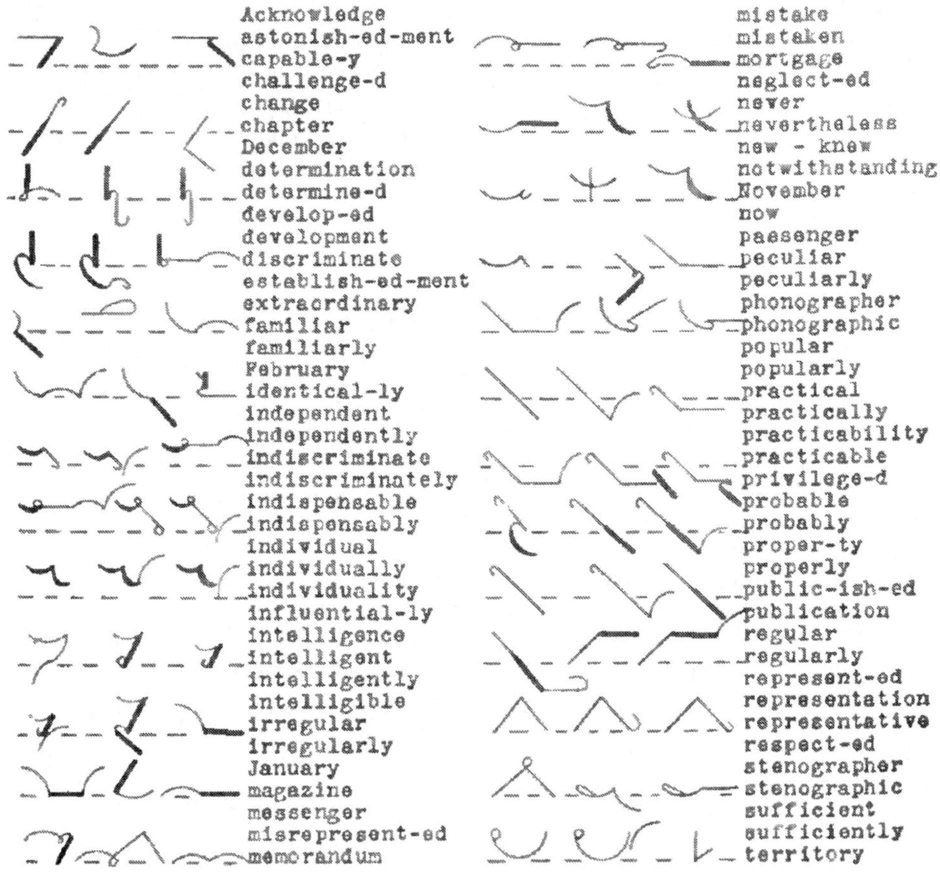

S I M P L E   P H R A S E S

The following phrases should be written again and again until ease and rapidity have been secured.

all right
anybody else
anything else
anything more
as far as
as fast as
as great as
as good as
as long as
as much as
as soon as
as soon as possible
as well as
as well as possible
as early as possible
as the
as follows
as near as you can
as has been
at the
at that
at owner's risk
at sender's risk
by the way
car load
carte blanche
dear sir
dear madam
dear friend
did you receive
did you mention
first place
first-class
for it is

for the matter
how many
has been
I am
I am afraid
I am certain
I am glad
I am very glad
(yours.
I am very truly
I am sure
I am surprised
I am sorry
I am very sorry
I have no doubt
I think so
I thank you
I shall be
I shall be glad
I shall not be
if he is
if the matter
if you can
if you cannot
if you can have
if it is possible
if it is to be
in answer
inasmuch as
in this city
in your city
in your place
in your letter
in the way
in the west

SIMPLE PHRASES -- Continued

Each time these phrases are written, they should be compared with the outlines given until they can be written without error.

in the country
in this country
in the manner
in the meantime
in the matter
in that matter
in this matter
in such
in such cases
is the
it has been
it is necessary
it is only
it seems to me
it would be
of course
of this date
on the
on cars
on track
on sale
per cent
per month
price list
price lists
such has been
that the
that is
thank you
that place
this place
this class
there is
there are

there has been
to some extent
to be able to
truly yours
very little
very likely
very truly
very truly yours
who is
with his
which would be
which would not be
will be satisfactory
we are
we will
we will be
we can
we can do
we can have
we cannot
we cannot have
we have
we have yours
we have your letter
we shall
we shall be
we are very truly (yours
your city
your place
your letter
you are in
you will be
you may have
you must

CONTRACTED PHRASES

Additional methods of phrasing will be found in the following list. The principles employed can be applied to other phrases, but the list embraces all that will be of special value.

at hand
is at hand
let us hear
let us know
let us proceed
have their-there
was there-their
was there anything
in their
know their
for there
for there is
if there is
if there is anything
receive their
when there is
whenever there is
I think there will be
I think there is
I am sure there is
our own
your own
their own
know their own
receive their own
at one
some one
every one
other than
more than
sooner than
faster than
less than
rather than
later than
further than
longer than
better than

greater than
in consideration
in order,-to
in receipt of,-the
in receipt of yours
I am in receipt of yours
I am in receipt of your letter
we are in receipt of,the
we are in receipt of yours
we are in receipt of your favor
in referring to,-the
in reference to,-the
in regard to,-the
in respect to,-the
in response to,-the
in reply to,-the
in reply to yours
in reply to your favor
in reply to your letter
in relation to,-the
yesterday morning
this morning
Monday morning
Tuesday morning
Wednesday morning
Thursday morning
Friday morning
Saturday morning
Sunday morning
at last
at least
at first
at any rate
at the same price
at the time
at the same time

CONTRACTED PHRASES - Continued

TABLE OF INITIAL AND FINAL BRIEF FORMS

	-S-	-SES-	-ST-	-STR	W-Y-	H-	-R	-L	-N	-FV	-TION	-TD	THER -TER -DER

A L P H A B E T I C A L   L I S T

of word signs and the words included in the special lists preceding.

A
accordance
account
acknowledge
addition
advance-d
advancement
advantage
advertise
advertised
advertises
afterward
agent
ago
ah
all
already
altogether
am
an
and
annual-ly
any
anybody
anyhow
anything
appear
apply
appropriate
appropriation
approve
are
as
assure
astonish-ed-ment
at all
at first
at hand
at length
at once
auditor
authority
aware
away
awe
balance
battery
be
been
because
become
before
began
begin
begun
behind
belief-believe

or

belong-ed
better
but
beyond
call
can
capable-y
careful-ly
challenge-d
change
chapter
character
characteristic
characterized
characters-ize
circumstance
circumstances
come
commence
commenced
commences
common
company
compassion
compliance
copy
consequent
constituent
could
count
credence
danger
daughter
dear
debtor
December
degree
deliver-y
describe-d
description
develop-ed
development
determination
determine-d
did not
differ-ent-ence
difficult-y
disadvantage
discriminate
do
do not
doctor
dollar
during
editor
enlarge-d

entire
equal-ly
equalization
establish-ed-ment
ever
every
extraordinary
eye
familiar
familiarly
favored
favorite
February
first
fiscal
follow
for
foreclose
foreclosure
forever
forward
from
general-ly
generals-ize
generalized
gentleman
gentlemen
give-n
good
govern-ed-ment
had
had not
half
hand
happen
happy
has
have
he
hereafter
hereinafter
herself
him
himself
his
hope
hope to have
how
however
hundred
I
identical-ly
imagine-ary-ation
immaterial
immediate-ly
important-ance
impossible-ility
improves
improve-d-ment
inconsiderate
independent
independently
indiscriminate
indiscriminately
indispensable
indispensably
individual
individually
individuality
inexperience
inexperienced
influence
influenced
influences
influential-ly
information
intelligence
intelligent
intelligently
intelligible
irregular
irregularly
is
issue
it
its
itself
January
knew
language
large
larger
largest
magazine
material-ly
member
memorandum
messenger
million
misrepresent-ed
mistake
mistaken
misunderstand
misunderstood
mortgage
more
Mr.
much
myself
nature
neglect-ed
never
nevertheless
new
next
nobody
notwithstanding
November
now
number
object
objection
objectionable
objective
occupy
of

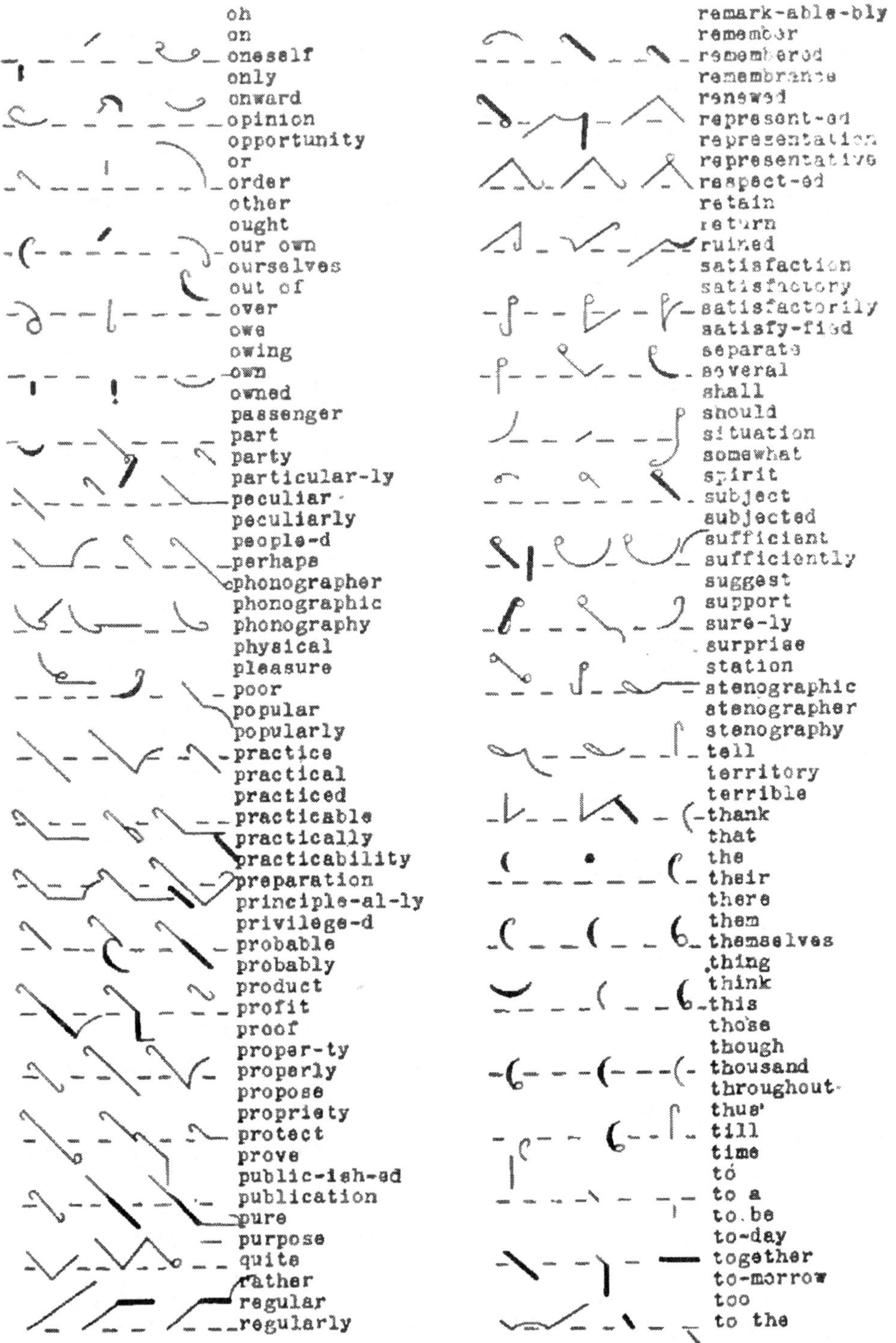
oh
on
oneself
only
onward
opinion
opportunity
or
order
other
ought
our own
ourselves
out of
over
owe
owing
own
owned
passenger
part
party
particular-ly
peculiar
peculiarly
people-d
perhaps
phonographer
phonographic
phonography
physical
pleasure
poor
popular
popularly
practice
practical
practiced
practicable
practically
practicability
preparation
principle-al-ly
privilege-d
probable
probably
product
profit
proof
proper-ty
properly
propose
propriety
protect
prove
public-ish-ed
publication
pure
purpose
quite
rather
regular
regularly
remark-able-bly
remember
remembered
remembrance
renewed
represent-ed
representation
representative
respect-ed
retain
return
ruined
satisfaction
satisfactory
satisfactorily
satisfy-fied
separate
several
shall
should
situation
somewhat
spirit
subject
subjected
sufficient
sufficiently
suggest
support
sure-ly
surprise
station
stenographic
stenographer
stenography
tell
territory
terrible
thank
that
the
their
there
them
themselves
thing
think
this
those
though
thousand
throughout
thus
till
time
to
to a
to be
to-day
together
to-morrow
too
to the

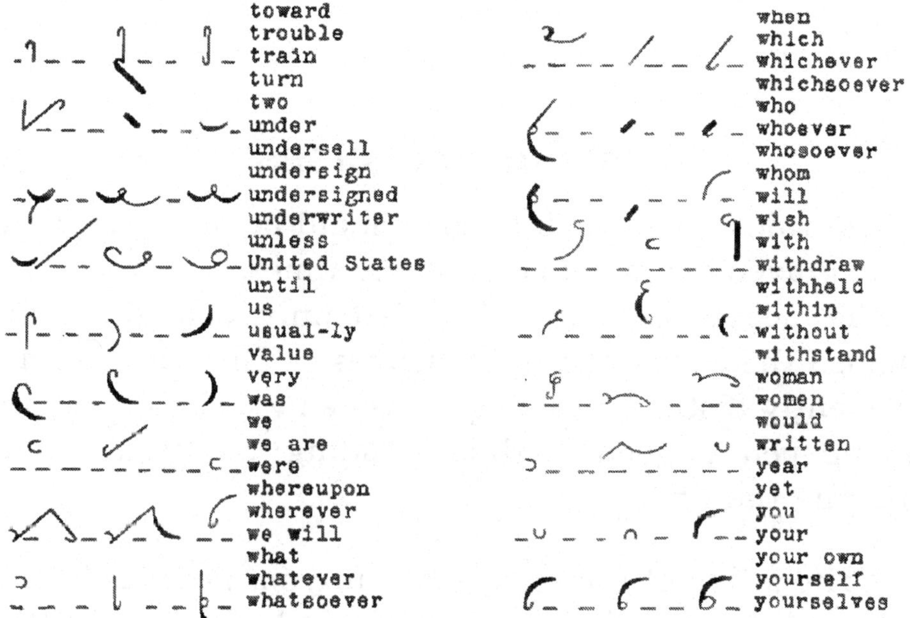
toward
trouble
train
turn
two
under
undersell
undersign
undersigned
underwriter
unless
United States
until
us
usual-ly
value
very
was
we
we are
were
whereupon
wherever
we will
what
whatever
whatsoever
when
which
whichever
whichsoever
who
whoever
whosoever
whom
will
wish
with
withdraw
withheld
within
without
withstand
woman
women
would
written
year
yet
you
your
your own
yourself
yourselves

WRITING EXERCISES

The rules under each lesson should be memorized and the engraved characters read many times.

The heavy strokes are shaded only enough to distinguish them from the light strokes. They can be made sufficiently distinct at a single stroke by a slight pressure on the pen or pencil, thus avoiding the necessity of retracing the line.

CONSONANTS

Write a line of each consonant in your note-book, first writing the name of the consonant in longhand. When each consonant has been written once show your note-book to the instructor, who will examine and date it. Then fill out the line and have it examined and dated again.

P, B, T, D, Chay, J, K, Gay, Ray, Hay, F, V, Ith, The, L, S, Z, Ish, Zhee, Lay, Yay, R, Way, M, Emp-Emb, N, Ing-Ink, T, V, M, Ray, Yay, Ish, P, J, R, Emp, B, K, The, N, Zhee, Lay, Z, Ith, D, Way, S, Gay, Ing, Chay, V, Ink, Emb, Hay, Z, B, Ing, The, Hay, R, Ith, D, Way, N, Emp, T, Ish, M, S, J, V, Emb, Ray, F, P, K, Chay, Zhee, Gay, Lay, Yay, Ink.

SEP 11 1905

First outline written ________ *Outlines completed* ________

CONSONANTS COMBINED

When consonants are joined, the first up or down stroke should rest upon the line. Combinations of horizontal consonants should rest upon the line. When two descending strokes are joined, the first rests upon the line and the second descends below it. Each outline must be carefully and accurately formed. All strokes must be of the same length.

R-R, Lay-Lay, N-D, K-B, N-B, K-J, N-Chay, P-Gay, Gay-P, Gay-T M-M, K-M, N-K, P-K, M-K, M-J, N-M, N-N, Lay-N, L-Ink, Emp-Ray, R-Emb, M-Ing, Lay-R, V-M, F-N, N-V, Chay-N, Gay-M, K-T, Chay-Gay, Gay-Chay, Ish-K, K-Ish, K-P, Hay-N, B-Ing, R-M, V-K-T, M-Gay-J, M-N-D, P-Ray-T, N-M-Lay, T-M-Ith, N-T-Ray, B-K-M, Ray-D-M, Ish-P-Lay, Emb-Lay-Ish, M-Ray-D, P-B-Lay-K, Lay-T-M-Lay, V-K-T-Ray.

SEP 13 1905

First outline written.................... *Outlines completed*...............

LONG VOWELS

Write all the consonants of a word before inserting the vowel or vowels. Each syllable of a word has but *one* vowel sound. In stenography, only the *sounds* of a word are expressed. When L is the only consonant stroke in the word, use *Lay*.

After the words have been written once, and the instructor has made the necessary corrections, carefully note them, and then fill out the line, following the same course as with the consonants.

WORDS: Ate, aid, aim, ace, bee, fee, thee, they, day, Coe, beau, eel, eke, ache, oak, eight, key, foe, Fay, gnaw, go, hoe, no, toe, jay, Joe, shoe, know, gay, Lou, law, ode, Lee, low, may, doe, way, neigh, awed, owed, ooze, oat, ease, paw, Poe, weigh, mow, saw, Shaw, show, woe, pay, so, say, nay, hay, woo, thaw, Abe, ale.

WORD SIGNS: The, a, ah, all, too-two, already, before, owe-oh, ought, who, whom.

First outline written SEP 1? 1905 *Outlines completed* SEP 1? 19

After the sentences have been written once and corrected by the instructor, each one should be written at least ten times. Two light ticks in the direction of *Chay* should be placed under a proper noun.

SENTENCES: 1. They may all go. 2 They already know the way. 3. They may see the Jew. 4. Each saw the show. 5 Who saw the bee? 6. All who ate may go. 7. Poe may weigh the hay. 8. Who saw the ode? 9. All who owe may pay. 10. Lee may aid Abe. 11. See the foe. 12. The toe may ache. 13. Fay may pay the fee. 14. Who saw me? 15. They who go may see all. 16. The beau may already be gay. 17. Ah, they may know all. 18. Who may own the hay? 19. They all say Coe may already know the law. 20. Before they go they may see the ape eat all the dough.

Sentences written once SEP 18 1905 *Sentences completed* SEP 18 19

A new lesson must not be taken up until the principles and practice-matter of the previous one have been *thoroughly* mastered. Especial attention should be given to the word signs, which are of the utmost importance.

SHORT VOWELS

Remember that each sign represents invariably the same sound, and that it is always written in the same direction, except the letter *l*; also that the first *ascending* or *descending* stroke in the outline is written in the position of the vowel in the *accented* syllable.

Doubt may sometimes arise regarding the use of the short second-place vowels; also regarding the use of the first and second-place heavy dash-signs. The distinct sounds in words of this class may be ascertained by reference to a standard dictionary. In writing shorthand, however, the exact distinction is hardly necessary.

Double consonants, as in Anna, dummy, muddy, etc., are expressed with but one stroke.

Words: Atom, adage, Anna, bush, botch, batch, ship, path, cop, choppy, check, dip, Dutch, dummy, ago, pad, Emma, fang, nook, gang, Gibb, gush, haughty, Havana, echo, jug, kink, knock, love, map, muddy, muff, many, manage, fathom, notary, income, engage, baggage, enigma, emanate, dignity, unpack, unmake, famish, avenge, becalm, entomb, fatigue, jockey, Panama, become, name, cheap, cash, money, baggage, pack, boat, dock, book, back, big, pick, thick, deck, beg, catch, tag, Canada.

Word Signs: An-and, of, to, to the, or, but, to a, on, should, how.

First outline written SEP 27 1905 *Outlines completed* OCT 12 1905

Sentences: 1. To whom should they go? 2. Take the cup to Minnie. 3. Who took the book back to the nook? 4. The boat may be at the beach before they know of it. 5. How may the money be paid to the Havana bank? 6. Fatigue may make me leave before Anna or Adam. 7. Many a month may go before they see it. 8. Take a big dish for the honey cake. 9. Make a cup of cocoa before they go back. 10. Hitch the gay nag to the buggy in the meadow. 11. Show Jennie how to pitch the penny to Tom. 12. But how should they see it if they go away? 13. Bob and Mamie may take the boat on the calm bay. 14. They ought to see the two sheep eat the hay. 15. All should go to Canada to catch fish. 16. They should manage to engage the boat. 17. Who ought to pay the money?

Sentences written once SEP 2[illegible] 1905 *Sentences completed* OCT 12 1905

DIPHTHONGS

Words: Dye, by, due, eyed, joy, lie, nigh, row, few, gouge, hide, ivy, fife, mouth, pouch, tube, fume, tiny, chime, tithe, toil, toiler, boyish, dower, Jewish, joyous, loyal, vial, theory, along, avail, borrow, abide, file, vile, revile, veil, failing, feeling, fur, hurry, jury, lame, lucky, lack, long, loop, booth, link, lung, mellow, Murray, namely, outlay, outlaw, par, ripe, rate, rink, review, renew, Raleigh, waylay, wring, wreath, tyro, early, pipe, couch, write, Rome, romp, mail, rail, empire, rare.

WORD SIGNS: I-eye, you, hope-happy-party, object-be, to be, time, it, dollar, do, had, which, much, advantage, large.

First outline written OCT 9 1905 *Outlines completed* OCT 16 1905

SENTENCES: 1 Do you know how to make money and how to keep it? 2. You may enjoy life if you know how to take advantage of it. 3. You should pay the bill which the party had to take. 4. Take the lower layer of the cake in the big dish. 5. Pack my bag full of food and take it to Tacoma. 6. Take the noisy boy to the shore to bathe in the sea. 7. Check the item on the bill before you go to the bank. 8. Ask the tailor to carry it to the polo game. 9. You may write out my idea now. 10. To be happy and live long you should do right. 11. I hope a dollar a day may be of advantage to all. 12. Of how much advantage may it be to each party? 13. They who borrow money should pay it back. 14. I may be in time to be of advantage to all. 15. I had to borrow a dollar to pay my bill. 16. Our object may be to see you pack the bag.

Sentences written out OCT 12 1905 *Sentences completed* OCT 16 1905

REVIEW WRITING EXERCISE.

WORDS: Aim, ahoy, ado, abbey, avow, Ann, Annie, anew, allay, ally, alley, alloy, adieu, aching, apathy, aiming, abode, alkali, bow, bag, bank, balky, babe, baby, bath, Booth, bang, balmy, boil, bug, buggy, beach, being, billow, balm, bedaub, botany, both, bathe, boat, coop, calm, choke, cheek, chub, chubby, chair, chum, cabbage, Choctaw, chiming, calk, chalk, coke, coach, cage, comb, came, chalky, Dey, dog, deep, dupe, damage, deify, downy, deem, dame, eighty, e l, Eli, etching, edging, epic, enigma, evoke, embalm, feud, fell, fall, far, folk, Fitchie, fagot, famish, foaming, fatigue, faith, fang, gawk, gig, gewgaw, game, gothic, Geneva, gape, infamy, jaggy, jog, jibe, Job, Jacob, Jamaica, knack, knew, lieu, levity, lady, manage, meadow, melody, monk, magic, mug, make, maim, monotony,

Mocha, myth, mouth, monk, monkey, mimic, mutiny, moth, Madonna, nag, new, nail, nabob, nib, nub, nymph, naming, Noah, Nero, Opie, off, oaf, owl, pew, pang, poke, patch, poach, papa, pop, pup, puppy, peep, peck, package, pagoda, Pope, palmy, thatch, tank, tooth, teeth, tame, teem, tar, thick, topic, tobacco, tomato, take, unfair, unmake, vail, veil, vivify, variety, vogue, viola.

First outline written.................... *Outlines completed*....................

SENTENCES: 1. You ought to see how much you owe before you go away. 2. You or I should see of how much advantage it may be. 3. It may be in time to be of advantage to all. 4. Who ought to go to the bank? 5. I am happy to say they may see it. 6. To whom should it be paid? 7. Do you know the advantage which may be in it? 8. How should I go to the rowing match in Canada? 9 My object may be to buy the large etching. 10. Which party ought to know of it?

Sentences written once.................... *Sentences completed*....................

CIRCLE S OR Z

WORDS: Sick, seat, suit, side, siege, scythe, safe, seen, sin, soon, same, seem, sway, case, keys, teas, days, does, dues, joys, ages, edges, ashes, these, office, face, voice, nice, ounce, knows, alms, house, yes, sets, seeks, space, seeking, speech, savage, Sunday, Smith, smoke, seeming, sinking, Thomas, annex, notice, anxious, annoyance, exceed, cousin, task, Tuesday, upset, passage, fasten, inside, insane, says, seize, spicy, access, vices, accuses, mazes, success.

WORD SIGNS: Is-his, as-has, subject, satisfy-fied, satisfactory, satisfactorily, several, advertise, advertises, because, this, thus-those, impossible-ility, improves, influence, influences.

First outline written.................... *Outlines completed*....................

SENTENCES: 1. James may arise early to see the sun rise 2. You may sell a dozen signs of this design. 3. You should advertise the notice in the daily Sun. 4. Miss Smith should make less noise at the show. 5. You may receive the offensive notice on Sunday. 6. Lucy asks if she may use my music box. 7. The assets of the bank are in excess of its losses. 8. I desire to know his reason to sell his houses. 9. If it is satisfactory you may advertise it now. 10. It is impossible to know its influence on the masses. 11. Miss Shaw possesses a nice voice to sing songs. 12. If the snow thaws, the seeds may be sown.

Sentences written once............*Sentences completed*............

LOOPS ST OR STR

If the sound of *st* or *str* precedes a final vowel sound, the loops cannot be used.

WORDS: Staid, august, paste, nest, hoist, guessed, Yost, soonest, safest, just, justice, stark, stork, solaced, fairest, forest, deepest, debased, fastest, funniest, stimulus, mustiest, repast, biggest, deduced, sticky, stubby, steamy, stuffy, stacks, stages, stakes, stalls, steals, stumps, stitches, stubs, stings, stores, stars, stairs, stole, styles, Hester, boaster, register, hoists, jests, feasts, lists, mists, baste, bastes, baster, boasters, jesters, coasters, posters, toasters, teamsters.

WORD SIGNS: Advertised, first, at first, largest, influenced, next, stenography.

Sentences written once............*Sentences completed*............

SENTENCES: 1. You should make haste slowly these chilly days. 2. Thomas lost the list of our stock of stoves. 3. The starch is sticky and may make the stuff too stiff. 4. Mary refused to receive the revised list of sales. 5. I am rejoiced to know of his arrest yesterday. 6. The minister may invest his money in stocks. 7. You may take the highway which goes to Worcester. 8. They may sell the rusty stove at the store. 9. The robust teamster may molest the gamesters at Rochester. 10. They should at first testify as to his unjust arrest. 11. You should at least be happy to possess it. 12. The next to the largest has influenced us.

Sentences written once............*Sentences completed*............

The *iss* circle, the *ist* loop, and the semicircles must be made very small.

WORDS: Widows, widower, wag, wink, war, windy, Edwin, wine, won, warehouse, work, wall, well, window, Wednesday, worst, Wheeling, wisp, stairway, Swiss, yes, yoke, yawn, youngest, twitch, dweller, quill, quit, quietly, qualm, queer, Quebec, unquiet, acquire, swing, Swede, squeak, squire, square, hem, hark, harem, hail, hill, help, hallow, holy, hale, haziness, whack, whiz, whistle, whisky, whip, whims, whiff, whittle, wheel, whine, feeling, failing.

In the middle of words, that form for *l* or *r* is used which makes the better angle with the preceding or following stroke. L, following the w-semicircle, must be written downward.

WORD SIGNS: He-him, we-with, were, what, would, year, yet, beyond, you, that, when, aware.

First outline written NOV 6 1905 *Outlines completed* NOV 6 190

SENTENCES: 1. The worst of the storm has now passed away. 2. Weave the wide web and you may receive wages. 3. Unyoke the oxen and they may go to the hedge 4. They may sell Tweed's dwelling house to Dwight. 5. Take the tweezers and twist the casters off the bureau. 6. Why do you wish to whistle here at this time? 7. The wheat may make white and wholesome hoe cakes. 8. We were all aware that you were in Wyoming. 9. The hammock is swung on the banks of the Wabash. 10. Why do you go to the game of whist with the whistler? 11. We were with you on last Wednesday at Owego. 12. You should be aware of it by th s time. 13. You should now write these items in the right way.

Sentences written once NOV 6 *Sentences completed* 6

The following writing exercises should not be taken up until the preceding ones have been thoroughly reviewed.

Do not combine words which join awkwardly. Join only words which are closely connected either naturally or grammatically. Do not try to form very long or complicated phrases.

Common words, such as *in*, *if*, *at*, *our*, *me*, *may*, *they*, *way*, *know*, *no*, *go*, *take*, *make*, *buy*, *these*, etc., may be written without vowels.

PHRASES: You will have, you are, you may, you must be, you must have; we think, we think you will, we shall have, we shall be; it is, it must, it must be, it must have, in that, that which, that which may, in his, if you will, if you will be; in these, in each, in this, in which, in those, in much, in each case, in which case; of it, to it, on it, should it, to have; I will be, I will have, I will do, I am sorry; I shall have, I shall be, I think you will be, I fear you will, I hope you will, I hope you may; have the, for the, in the, take the, by the way, in the way, in the west; we will be, we will have, we will do, we are in, we are sorry; you will, I will, we will, he will, they will.

Sentences written once............ *Sentences completed*..............

SENTENCES: 1. It is of common advantage to give it together. 2. The company will come for half an hour. 3. Have they given it to us, or are you going to do so? 4. Have you ever seen them do so? 5. I will thank them a thousand times for it. 6. I think, however, it will be to our advantage. 7. We shall issue our usual important book this year. 8. Your language will make us go away soon. 9. Is the thing of any importance to our own case? 10. I think you would be sorry if we should go with them. 11. You must in each case do as we desire. 12. I hope you will have no wish to do so. 13. If you will take the road to the west you will be all right. 14. In this case I shall be happy to have you sing the song. 15. We will have the improvement ready by the 15th of May.

Sentences written once............ *Sentences completed*..............

The *r* hook in the middle of an outline sometimes cannot be perfectly formed, in which case it is retraced on the preceding stroke. In the middle of outlines the circle must be made on the *inside* of the hook on straight strokes.

Mer and *Emper* cannot be used after *T*, *D*, *Chay*, and *J*.

WORDS: Drape, drag, grape, trail, thrash, caprice, pauper, approach, dapper, daughter, hammer, banner, camphor, favors, traverse, cracker, abridge, authority, scrap, abstruse, creek, freak, shred, decrease, generous, Denver, educator, embrace, pressure, precede, trespass, treason, reproach, redress, presence, treasure, setter, scream, chemistry, tribe, crib, fiber, spider, diagram, silver, Fisher, triumph, increase, strips, industry, dishonor, broil, prop, prong, broth, broom, growl, throb, brother, lumber, thinker, anger, proceed, grocer, soldier, program, oppressive, strong, scroll, rumor, lunar, crusade, numerous, quaver, crutch, ludicrous, trustee, succor, supremacy, supersede, lustrous, quarter, quarterly, crystal, university, Friday, dexterous, extremity, seamstress.

WORD SIGNS: Appear, principle-al-ly, practice, member-remember, number, doctor, dear, during, danger, larger, degree, from.

First outline written.................... *Outlines completed*..........

SENTENCES: 1. The preacher was eager to preach at Troy on Thursday. 2. The robber caused much labor and bother for us. 3. The shipper will protest that the wharfage was extra. 4. They must try to escape from the State prison. 5. Doctor Baker and his brother have the principal practice there. 6. It appears that they must pay the next quarter's dues. 7. The industrious baker is extremely generous. 8. The members agree to all that we require. 9. The doctor was away during the danger of the fever. 10. They may ship the paper and crackers by the next express. 11. The subscribers disagree with the editor of the paper. 12. The lumber fell on the younger brother's finger and broke it. 13. The baker and the banker must purchase a banner and wave it.

Sentences written once .... Sentences completed ....

THE L HOOK

The *r* hook must always be made very small, so that it may not conflict with the *l* hook on curved letters.

WORDS: Clause, glass, pliable, blemish, clump, climax, clothe, clumsy, Clara, clog, closed, glares, gleam, glum, glimpse, flake, flimsy, Florida, fling, fluency, flabby, flogs, papal, pebble, entitle, beetle, cackle, chattel, fickle, giggle, plumper, blank, circle, declaim, diploma, employ, emblem, enclose, festival, syllable, radical, tenable, technical, poetical, parable, novelty, admirable, variable, vital, splices, penal, diagonal, amicable, bashful, chemical, declivity, temporal, spinal, joyful, reliance, pliable, shingle, survival, wrinkle, implore, desirable, ramble, explicable, invaluable, paternal, warble, criminal, problem, chronicle, struggle, scruple, perplex.

WORD SIGNS: People-d, apply, belong-ed, at all-until, deliver-y, equal-ly difficult-y, follow, value.

First outline written *Outlines completed*

SENTENCES: 1. To whom does the black cloak belong? 2. I will enclose an envelope. 3 Flora was the only girl in the class who pleased the teacher. 4. We are now able to display our flag in all climes. 5. You may receive the reply by cable to-morrow. 6 The clock was placed in the chapel to tell the time. 7. The classical pupil must apply at the uni ersity. 8. The faculty was in the assembly hall on Friday. 9. The title to the tunnel was official, but it was of no value 10. You must settle for the supply of satchels when they are placed on sale. 11. The clause in the classics pleases the pupils of all classes.

Sentences written over .... Sentences completed ..

THE N HOOK

The hook forms cannot be used before a final vowel. In the middle of outlines the circle must be made on the *inside* of the hooks on straight strokes.

WORDS: Pin, chin, grown, spin, stain, sudden, seven, widen, downs, chance, instance, assistance, expanse, bounce, bounced, bounces, bouncer, dispenses, responses, dampen, barren, famine, deepen, enjoin, refine, bench, vacancy, penny, Vienna, rainy, fans, earns, offense, offenses, whitens, sponsor, bunch, finances, leaner, occupancy, punish, mince, nuns, canes, dense, duns, tons, abstain, arraign, assign, assignee, aspen, button, campaign, cheapen, detain, discern, engine, examine, foreign, hidden, humane, illumine, Japan, lemon, oranges, linen, machine, stiffen, stolen, summon, sullen, thine, turn, wagon, weapon, whetstone, woven, bonny, Illinois, hempen, Spanish, zones, gunnery, soften, enhance.

Puff, beef, reef, rebuff, tariff, sheriff, pave, repave, bereave, coffee, purify, verify, Java, defeat, refer, recovery, devote, river, puffs, achieves, heaves.

WORD SIGNS: General-ly, can, begin, phonography, opinion, our own, your own, at length, at once, generals-ize, generalized, remembrance, differ-ent-ence, advance-d, careful-ly, hope to have, whatever, out of, whichever, whoever.

First outline written.................. *Outlines completed*..................

SENTENCES: 1. Will you join in the fun down town at seven o'clock? 2. John Shane will assign his stock to his assignee. 3. Refine the iron, and finish it within twenty days. 4. I incline to make many bayonets for use in Oregon. 5. The chances for making your expenses in Kansas are slim. 6. The finances of the bank in this financial strain have increased. 7. The expenses of the princes at the dances were out of all reason. 8. They announce that he evinces many signs against the loans. 9. It is your opinion that they will begin work at once. 10. I observe that he refers to the discovery of the reef. 11. The sensitive man has no incentive to refuse the trophy. 12. You may refuse to revise his defense at the trial. 13. As a general thing you can begin the study of phonography in your own town. 14. Our own opinion is that whatever is done you will hear at once. 15. The general's remembrance of it will at length be right. 16. Whoever goes should be careful to come out of it in time. 17. Whatever difference there is, and whichever way you go, it will be our gain.

Sentences written once FEB 8 1906 *Sentences completed* FEB 8 1906

THE SHUN HOOK

WORDS: Omission, ovation, sedition, collision, partition, vocation, mention, dictation, selection, legation, pollution, locomotion, ascension, aspiration, digression, abolition, violation, division, passionate, stationary, missionary, reception, inception, obligation, benediction, discretion, attrition, creation, suction, affliction, prostration, production, abbreviation, dissipation, presumption, superstition, exclusion, designation, emigration, expedition, exclamation, expiration, exultation, subscription, exploration, execution, passions, auctions, mentions, affections, sessions, fashions, deceptions, locations, resolutions.

Civilization, deposition, exposition, succession, taxation, dispensation, secession, vexation, musicians, decisions, positions, possessions.

WORD SIGNS: Objection, information, satisfaction, description, from, over, very, there-their, other, sure-ly, pleasure, Mr-remark-able-bly, more, describe-d, practiced, character, characters, characterized, characteristic.

First outline written .... *Outlines completed* ....

SENTENCES: 1. It is the intention to give an option on sales at the auction. 2. I have a notion that education is a delusion. 3. The national ambition is to have attention given to the operation. 4. He sanctions their actions for the nation's progress. 5. There is opposition to the possession of our new acquisitions. 6. The decision of the musicians for a cessation of the play gives satisfaction. 7. What objection is there to the information if it gives satisfaction? 8. The description he receives from them is very fine. 9. We surely had much pleasure from his remark on this occasion. 10. Their sessions were more noisy than is usually the case. 11. Is there to be any motion from the other side? 12. Mr. Brown and Mr. Jones will surely be there on that occasion. 13. They had more pleasure from his remarks than from others. 14. If you will pay attention to the directions you will be master of the situation.

Sentences written once .... *Sentences completed* ....

HALF LENGTH STROKES

A half length stroke cannot precede a final vowel sound. A *compound* character is one used with the *semi-circle* or with an *initial* or *final* hook.

Pat, cheat, coat, feat, meet, mate, not, shut, sipped, soaked, soft, smite, skate, slate, cats, fights, hacked, good, bids, saved, reach, reached, bake, baked, vivid, rigid, argued, aimed, made, mode, seemed, end, send, sound, signed, sinned, doomed, timid, descend, Pratt, street, sobered, blade, tend, attend, mound, brought, great, greatly, ascertained, attract, October, abound, enchant, Kentucky, resume, scold, framed, field, veiled, absurd, whetted, payment, print, reeled, ruled, crate, create, pot, poet, endued, endowed, invite, invited, headed, padded, faded, derived, divided, shrouded, righted, pickled, bottled, tackled, awaited, dieted, unedited, agitated, ray, raid, raided, radiate, radiated, inundated, Benedict, acted, dated, freighted.

Doing, making, saying, having, missing, hopping, aiding, abusing, tracing; ravings, sayings, ratings, openings; watching the, dividing the, mocking the, arranging the; feasibility, invisibility, visibility, mutability, temporality, totality, circularity, muscularity, vulgarity.

WORD SIGNS: Particular-ly, opportunity, part, remembered, at hand, did not, do not, had not, gentlemen, gentleman, quite, could, good, that, without, immediate-ly, under, hand-owned, somewhat.

Outlines written once .... *Outlines completed* ....

SENTENCES: 1. In spite of the fight he sent the mat late last night. 2. He vowed that the deed would be void if not sent soon 3. The talkative man went to the tent and betrayed the band. 4. You should take pride in the gift sent by the general. 5 The noted man who offended us will be avoided. 6. He edited the report which was dated last week. 7. They are thinking of trying to buy the shining cup. 8. They are speaking of paying for the drawings. 9. The engravings will be shown at the meetings of the society. 10. We did not know because we had not heard of it. 11. His responsibility and popularity are very great because of his prosperity. 12. I remember that we had a particularly good opportunity without his aid. 13. We did not know that the gentleman was at hand at that time. 14. He said that part of it would be sent immediately to the shipper. 15. If he made it wrong that will be the end of it.

Sentences written once——— *Sentences completed*———

DOUBLE LENGTH STROKES

WORDS: Fighter, latter, mutter, shouter, flutter, flitter, alter, softer, smatter, salter, saunter, sender, surrender, cinder, matters, slanders, shatters, enters, finder, vendor, asunder, lender, whiter, yonder, wonder, hinder, islander, flounder, mentor, warder, astral, inventor, thermometer, defrauder, smelter, disorder, provender, intercept, interfere, interrupt, interdict, interest, introduce, entertain, entertained.

Concede, conceit, conceive, concise, concur, condemn, condense, confine, consent, consign, contract, convince, conception, conclusion, combination, comfort, commend, communication, communicate, compel, competent, comply, accommodate, discontinue, inconvenient, reconsider, intercommunication, circumvent, self-educated, self-support, insert, insertion, insulation, magnifiable, magnetic, countersign, contradict, controversy.

WORD SIGNS: Material, immaterial, commence, commenced, commences-United States, circumstance, circumstances, inexperience, inexperienced.

Outline written once——— *Outlines completed*———

SENTENCES: 1. I shall write a letter to father and mother about it. 2. The diameter of the meters is another matter. 3. The voters were in the center of the fighters. 4 The cylinder was too slender for the shutters. 5. I must confess that I did not consider your communication. 6. I have concluded that the condition of the concern is contrary to good order. 7. In recognition of the compensation received I will recommend you to the committee. 8. It is self-evident that his self-respect is an inspiration. 9. We must circumvent them and be self-possessed. 10. The instrument was an inspiration to all who heard it. 11. The magnificent scene could not be too greatly magnified. 12 It is immaterial when you commence to ship the motors. 13. Under the circumstances we will not consider his inexperience. 14. The United States possess material for all purposes. 15. It is an experienced man who has commenced to render their accounts.

*Sentences written once*____________ *Sentences completed*____________

CPSIA information can be obtained
at www.ICGtesting.com
Printed in the USA
LVOW03s1327070116
469659LV00014B/300/P